Every Day with Jesus
MAR/APR 2018

GW00888751

A Higher Love

'Many waters cannot quench love;
rivers cannot wash it away.'
Song of Songs 8:7

Selwyn Hughes
Revised and updated by Mick Brooks

© CWR 2017. Dated text previously published as *Every Day with Jesus: The Beloved* (March/April 2000) by CWR.
This edition revised and updated for 2018 by Mick Brooks.

CWR, Waverley Abbey House, Waverley Lane, Farnham, Surrey GU9 8EP, UK **Tel: 01252 784700**
Email: mail@cwr.org.uk Registered Charity No. 294387. Registered Limited Company No. 1990308.

MIX
Paper from
responsible sources
FSC® C015900

Every Day with Jesus is available in large print from CWR. It is also available on **audio and DAISY** in the UK and Eire for the sole use of those with a visual impairment worse than N12, or who are registered blind. For details please contact **Torch Trust for the Blind**, Tel: 01858 438260. Torch House, Torch Way, Northampton Road, Market Harborough LE16 9HL.

A word of introduction...

I confess I do enjoy a compelling bit of television – especially documentaries, and none so much as *24 Hours in A&E*. It's a UK fly-on-the-wall series that follows the comings and goings of a busy London hospital emergency department, for a single period of 24 hours. Cameras everywhere record life as it happens. As the opening credits roll, the narrator's voice calmly introduces 'love, life and loss, all in 24 hours'. Various team members, from consultants to receptionists, share their observations of this crucible of human emotion and experience. One nurse comments: 'the moment you're in Resus and really sick, all you can think about is, "Am I going to live or die?" Silly things go out the window, and ultimately, what's important is realised – "Am I loved?" and "Am I alone?"'

These powerful questions always strike me forcibly. They beautifully sum up the heart of the gospel and the heart of God. We are loved, and we are not alone. Life can be extraordinarily difficult, but I have learned that we can face anything when we know that we are not alone and we are loved.

The life-changing truth of this is the theme of this issue. God *is* love. His ultimate goal is that we would know Him and be known to Him – walking each day, *every day*, with Jesus. This Easter, whatever your situation, know this: you are loved and not alone.

Mick

Mick Brooks, Consulting Editor

We are His lovers

FOR READING & MEDITATION – COLOSSIANS 3:1–17

*'as God's chosen people, holy and dearly loved, clothe yourselves
with compassion, kindness, humility' (v12)*

We begin today a theme that touches on a mostly neglected subject in Christian circles – the passionate yet tender love that lies at the heart of the Trinity. This is brought out over and over again in Scripture, but so little seems to be made of it in our preaching and writing (and perhaps I've been as guilty of that as anyone). Nothing brings this truth home to our spirits more powerfully than the fact that God refers to His chosen people in all-embracing, intimate, loving terms.

The New King James Version translates today's text as: 'Therefore as the elect of God, holy and beloved'. What a tender ring there is in the word 'beloved'. In my view, it's a pity that the NIV has dropped the word 'beloved' from this and similar texts. The NIV, referring to God's love for His people, uses the word 'beloved' just twice (Deut. 33:12; Jer. 11:15). Perhaps the translators of the NIV regarded the word 'beloved' as belonging to another generation, but I believe the word still has a place today, and this is the term I shall be using throughout these meditations to describe the way in which God looks upon His redeemed children.

FURTHER STUDY

Deut. 33;
Jer. 11:15

1. Write a definition of the word 'beloved'.

2. What do you think of Lady Julian's conclusion?

Lady Julian of Norwich was once given a series of revelations into the sufferings of Christ and the wonder of the gospel. She was taken into the heart of God and came away with this simple conclusion: 'We are not just the object of His care and concern – we are His lovers'. According to Charles Finney, love is 'bringing about the highest good in the life of another – that is the kind of love God has for us'. Divine love, however, also carries passionate yet tender elements. God is passionate about His relationship with His people. We are beloved.

Dear Father, help me to understand that the relationship You long to have with me is a passionate, intimate one. I know that You are what my heart longs for. I praise Your holy name. Amen.

The top of the scale

FOR READING & MEDITATION – PSALM 36:1–12

'How priceless is your unfailing love! Both high and low among men find refuge in the shadow of your wings.' (v7)

We continue laying down the amazing truth that God loves us with passionate, loving, tender care, and He looks upon us – His people – as His lovers. In their book *The Sacred Romance*, Brent Curtis and John Eldridge help us to notice that Scripture uses a wide range of metaphors to describe our relationship to God, which they interestingly place in an ascending order. Near the 'bottom', they say, we are seen as clay and He the potter. Then, as we rise higher, we are described as the sheep and He is the shepherd. Moving upward still, we are pictured as servants, and He is the master. Most of us, they suggest, never get past this point. But moving up higher still, we are described as God's children. But, they say, we can go up to a higher level still – the level where God calls us His 'friends'.

FURTHER STUDY

Gen. 1; 2

1. How does Genesis show humans as the pinnacle of creation?

2. Why did God create Eve after Adam?

Is there anything higher? Yes, say these writers. At the top of the scale there is a level of intimacy awaiting us that those hearing of it for the first time can hardly take in – we are His lovers. The relationship the Trinity longs to have with us is most definitely an intimate one. But at the same time, God longs for a relationship where His love for us is reciprocated by our love for Him.

Yesterday I quoted the words of Lady Julian of Norwich that 'we are His lovers'. I once repeated that to a man I was counselling. 'Ah,' he said, 'that is a woman talking – a single woman; that kind of imagery fails to capture the heart of a man.' Well, that kind of imagery certainly captures my heart and, I am sure, the hearts of many other men. I have no hesitation in saying that I fell in love with Jesus Christ many years ago – and I haven't got over it yet.

Jesus, lover of my soul, how can I thank You enough for loving me the way You do? Take me deeper into that love and give me an ever growing consciousness of its length and breadth and depth and height. Amen.

Living from the heart

FOR READING & MEDITATION – PSALM 48:1–14

'Within your temple, O God, we meditate on your unfailing love.' (v9)

Yesterday we referred to the comment of a man who had difficulty in seeing God as a passionate lover. 'That kind of imagery,' he said, 'fails to capture the heart of a man.' I wondered how much defensiveness lay behind his view, and I later found out. Brought up in a home where affectionate love was never demonstrated, he found it difficult to relate to his wife or even to talk to her in loving or tender terms. So it was little wonder he found the thought of a loving relationship with Jesus somewhat alien or intimidating.

I have met many men who because of culture, poor parental modelling, or deep hurts in the area of love, find it difficult to admit to or express any feelings of love that they might experience. One man said to me: 'It would be easier for me to fly to the moon than to express romantic feelings of love towards my wife.' When I was conducting a marriage seminar, another man said to me: 'There are times when I feel so loving towards my wife that I almost tell her!' Thankfully, not all men are like that!

One of my privileges as a counsellor has been to look into the souls of thousands of men, and I have seen there a desire to live from the heart and experience a loving relationship with Jesus as much as in the heart of women. It might sound strange to non-Christians, or even new Christians, to hear a man say in his prayers, 'I love You, Lord'. My dictionary says that 'romantic' means 'being touched deeply in the imaginative and emotional part of one's life'. Can anything touch our emotions more deeply than the truth that we are loved by the world's most forceful lover? Men as well as women can say 'Amen' to that.

FURTHER STUDY

Psa. 31:21–24; 107; 136

1. What motivated the psalmist to write?

2. Meditate on the phrase 'His love endures forever'.

Father, nothing fills my heart with such wonder and emotion as the knowledge that I am loved by You. May that wonder increase. In Jesus' name. Amen.

Love that knows no fear

FOR READING & MEDITATION – 1 JOHN 4:7–21

'There is no fear in love. But perfect love drives out fear,
because fear has to do with punishment.' (v18)

We said yesterday that some men, for various reasons, find it difficult to come to terms with the truth that God desires to have an intimate relationship with His people. They might hesitate at a description of God being, as one writer puts it, an Ageless Romancer. But this problem is not limited only to men; some women experience it too. I have counselled many women who have had a fear of anything intimate. They could handle the idea of love in general, but the thought of being vulnerable to someone in a romantic sense was greatly threatening.

FURTHER STUDY

Psa. 3; 27; 91; 118

1. What is the root of fear?

2. What is the root of fearlessness?

One reason that people shrink from an intimate relationship with someone is the fear of being out of control – and underlying all fear is a lack of trust. Whatever you can't trust you tend to be afraid of, so a defence mechanism develops: 'when afraid, avoid'. Usually, hurts or injuries to the soul in the early developmental years are the roots of this condition – things like abuse, strong manipulative parent–child relationships, and so on. Good counselling, however, can help to overcome this problem.

If you are someone who recoils from the whole idea of an intimate relationship, then remember this: you have no reason to mistrust the love that flows out of the heart of God for you. None of the members of the Trinity will ever mistreat you, manipulate you or do anything to harm you. They love you, not for what you can give them, but simply because they delight in what they have to give to you. Whatever may have caused you to be afraid of love, you will find none of those things in the heart of the Trinity. As an old hymn puts it: 'Have no fear, perfect love is near'.

Father, whatever fears may be in my heart that prevent me opening up to You in absolute trust, help me grasp that I can wholly trust You. Help me to dissolve all my fears in Your perfect love. Amen.

CWR Ministry Events

PLEASE PRAY FOR THE TEAM

DATE	EVENT	PLACE	PRESENTER(S)
1 Mar	Sharing Jesus	Waverley Abbey House	Andy Peck
5–9 Mar	Woman to Woman	WAH	Inspiring Women team
8 Mar	Refreshing Your Spiritual Life	WAH	Andy Peck
15 Mar	Pastoring Through Crises	WAH	Andy Peck
16 Mar	Pastoral Care From Scratch	WAH	Andy Peck
19–23 Mar	Introduction to Biblical Care and Counselling	WAH	John Munt and team
23–25 Mar	Bible Discovery Weekend	WAH	Philip Greenslade
18 Apr	Inspiring Women Spring Day: Walking Strong in the Name of God, Every Day	WAH	Ros Derges and Lynette Brooks
19 Apr	Developing Your Small Group Strategy	WAH	Andy Peck
28 Apr	Insight into Self-Esteem	WAH	Chris Ledger

Please pray for our students and tutors on our ongoing BA Counselling programme at Waverley Abbey College (which takes place at Waverley Abbey House and Pilgrim Hall), as well as our Certificate in Christian Counselling and MA Counselling qualifications.

We would also appreciate prayer for our ongoing ministry in Singapore and Cambodia, as well as the many regional events that will be happening around the UK this year.

For further information and a full list of CWR's courses, seminars and events, call (+44) 01252 784719 or visit www.cwr.org.uk.courses

You can also download our free Prayer Track, which includes daily prayers, from www.cwr.org.uk/prayer-track

Reason enough

FOR READING & MEDITATION – DEUTERONOMY 7:1–11

'But it was because the LORD loved you... that he brought you out with a mighty hand and redeemed you' (v8)

Some people struggle with the fact that God loves them – not because of a fear of love, but because they feel unworthy of it. Many years ago, someone I was counselling burst into tears when I began to explore how they were loved deeply by God. When I asked why they were crying, they replied, 'I can't think of a single reason why God should love me.' I picked up a Bible and shared the passage that is before us today. Moses was telling the people of Israel that they were not chosen because of any merit in them but, 'because the LORD loved you'. I said: 'There may not be any logical reason why God should love you. He loves you because He simply can't help loving you.' The hymn writer Charles Wesley once looked for reasons why God should love him. Finding no logical reason for it, he put it like this: 'He has loved... He has loved me... I cannot tell why.'

FURTHER STUDY

Rom. 9:14–16;
1 Cor. 1:26–31;
Titus 3:3–7

1. What initiates God's love for us?

2. Complete the sentence: 'God loves me because...'

'The heart,' said the French mathematician and philosopher Blaise Pascal, 'has reasons that the head knows nothing about.' So don't look for logical reasons as to why God loves you. Accept the fact that there may not be any logic to it. Nothing in you gave rise to it, and nothing in you can extinguish it. Love, you see, is not arguable. If you look for a reason, you will most probably not find one. God says, 'I love you... because... I would love.' God loves us and delights in us not for any reason but because that's who He is. So the next time you ask, 'Jesus, what possible reason can you have for loving me?', don't be surprised if you hear nothing more than the word 'because'. Let that be reason enough.

Father, what assurance it gives me to know that Your love for me is not dependent on my love for You. My love goes up and down; Your love stays strong and constant. This truth makes me want to love You more. Thank You, my Father. Amen.

Crazy about you

FOR READING & MEDITATION – ISAIAH 62:1–12

*'They will be called... The Redeemed of the Lord; and you will be
called Sought After, The City No Longer Deserted.' (v12)*

We continue exploring the thought of God being an Ageless Romancer. Perhaps nothing is more pleasing than the thought that we are pursued. In the passage before us today, Isaiah gives a cluster of new names for the people of God: 'Holy People, The Redeemed, Sought After, The City No Longer Deserted'. Note the words 'Sought After'. God loved the children of Israel and longed so much for a close relationship with them that He continually pursued them; whenever they ran away from Him, He ran after them. That is how I believe He looks upon you and me – His present-day children. We also are a people 'sought after' or 'pursued'. This is part of our role in God's great story. We are the pursued – the beloved. If that is not an exciting thought, then tell me what is!

I know of nothing in this world that can enable a Christian to feel more secure in the midst of insecurity than the truth that we are part of a sacred romance. The God of the universe has gone to the utmost lengths to capture our hearts. George Herbert put it like this:

> *My God what is a heart*
> *That Thou shouldst it so eye and woo*
> *Powering upon it with all Thy art,*
> *As if Thou hadst nothing else to do.*

So drop your anchor into the depths of this reassuring and encouraging revelation today. You are the object of God's tender yet passionate love. God is simply crazy about you.

FURTHER STUDY

Gen. 24; 29:1–30

1. How does Genesis 24 illustrate the gospel?

2. In what way is Jacob a 'type' of Christ?

My Father and my God, my heart rejoices in the fact that I am caught up in a sacred romance. You feel passionate about Your relationship with me. May I be as passionate about my relationship with You. In Jesus' name I pray. Amen.

Nothing else matters

FOR READING & MEDITATION – HOSEA 11:1–11

'My heart is changed within me; all my compassion is aroused.' (v8)

We saw yesterday that we are the pursued – the beloved. The writers I referred to a few days ago, Brent Curtis and John Eldridge, wrote: 'few have ever felt pursued... sometimes we wonder if we've even been noticed. Father was too busy to come to our games, or perhaps he jumped ship altogether. Mother was lost in a never-ending pile of laundry... It is a rare soul indeed who has been sought after for who [they are] not because of what [they] can do.' They go on to illustrate that those who don't feel pursued often feel they have no value or worth.

FURTHER STUDY

Ezek. 34:11–16;
Matt. 23:37;
Luke 15:1–10;
19:1–10;
Gen. 6:6

1. Do you think God has pursued you?

2. Does Scripture teach that God is passionate?

Everyone longs to be loved. When we are not, we are tempted to say to ourselves, 'There must be something wrong with me, something dark and unlovable inside.' This is one of the biggest obstacles counsellors face: people who, because they did not feel loved in their developmental years or were not pursued, come to view themselves as being unworthy of love. Let it stagger you if you will, but this is the exciting truth – though no one may have pursued you on this earth, you have been pursued by the eternal God. The Ageless Romancer has set His love upon you. You are loved, and loved passionately.

The doctrine of God's impassibility has sometimes been misunderstood to mean God has no feelings; that His love is purely an action of the will. It is true that the Greek word *agape* conveys love in action, but we are wrong to think of it as containing no feeling. In certain types of relationships, passionate love is called for – and that is the kind of relationship God has with His redeemed people.

Father, I never cease to wonder at the fact of Your relentless pursuit of me. Whomever else may not love me, You love me. Nothing else matters. Amen.

Feelings that brim over

FOR READING & MEDITATION – JEREMIAH 31:1–14

'The LORD appeared to us in the past, saying: "I have loved you with an everlasting love; I have drawn you with loving-kindness."' (v3)

Those who believe that God is without feelings may have great difficulty with today's passage. The words brim over with feeling. And note the use of sensual metaphors: 'you will be rebuilt, O Virgin Israel' (v4). Let's not be troubled by the intimate language that Scripture uses to describe the relationship between God and His people. As one commentator says: 'Metaphors that are rich with sexual connotations are often used to summarise humanity's unwillingness and inability to sustain a loyal relationship with a faithful God. The well-known disturbance and corruption in the relationships of the sexes is used to describe the sin-crossed relations of people with God. The work of salvation takes place in the ruins of broken commitments and the rubble of deteriorated loyalties.'

FURTHER STUDY

Ezek. 16:1–34; Hosea 1 & 2

1. How do sexual relationships mirror God and His people?

2. Why does God use these particular illustrations?

God, when speaking through the prophets, often used sexual metaphors to identify the sins of the people. In the seventh century BC, Jeremiah said, 'you have the brazen look of a prostitute' (Jer. 3:3). And Ezekiel, in the sixth century BC, uses sexual language to describe God's relationship with Israel: 'when I… saw that you were old enough for love, I spread the corner of my garment over you and covered your nakedness. I gave you my solemn oath and entered into a covenant with you… and you became mine' (Ezek. 16:8).

Why is such intimate phraseology used like this, particularly as it relates to God's love for us? Is God a sexual being? No, He is not. These vivid and descriptive word pictures bring home to us most powerfully that God is passionate about His relationship with us. And the way He loves us is the way He wants us to love Him – passionately.

Father, forgive me for the coldness of my love. Stir up within my heart a love that echoes Your love for me. Help me, Lord. In Jesus' name. Amen.

Check your prayer life

FOR READING & MEDITATION – PHILIPPIANS 1:1–11

*'And this is my prayer: that your love may abound more and more
in knowledge and depth of insight' (v9)*

Yesterday we discussed God's use of sexual metaphors to illustrate the intimacy He has with His redeemed people. Eugene Peterson writes of a woman who came to him for counselling. Her first remark was: 'Well I guess you want to know all about my sex life – that's what they always want to know.' Peterson replied: 'If that's what you want to talk about, I'll listen. What I would be really interested in finding out about, though, is your prayer life.' Why would he say that? Because Peterson knew, as experienced pastors and counsellors know, that one of the ways to find out how a person handles intimate relationships is to ask them to talk about their prayer life.

FURTHER STUDY

Isa. 61:10–11;
Psa. 45;
John 17

1. How are sexuality and prayer linked?

2. How is Jesus' relationship with God expressed through prayer?

Non-Christian counsellors need to explore a person's sex life to explore how they handle relationships; a Christian counsellor need only ask how the person uses the language of prayer. Peterson says, 'Sexuality and prayer criss-cross constantly in pastoral work; they are both aspects of a single created thing – a capacity for intimacy.' Both can be explored to understand how a person relates to another at the deepest level of relationship.

What is your prayer life like, I wonder? Dull or dynamic? Passionate or prosaic? When we express our love for another person, we use the same words, actions and emotions that we use in the expression of our love for God. A person who is inhibited in the way they express love to another person will usually be inhibited in the way they express love to God. Take an in-depth look over the next few days at your prayer life. You might discover something about yourself that I hope will not just challenge you but change you.

Father, do not withhold anything from me. If You see I need heart surgery, I give You permission, for Your hands are healing. Help me to be open, both to myself and You. In Jesus' name I ask it. Amen.

Spreading **HOPE**
this Easter...

In partnership with Prison HOPE, CWR has recently published *40 Stories of Hope* – a collection of 40 remarkable testimonies from prisoners, ex-offenders and prison chaplains about life-changing encounters with Jesus. So far, over 15,000 copies have been sent into prisons for use during Lent – so today, thousands of people both in and out of prison will be reading about the unconditional love and hope that Jesus offers.

For every copy of *40 Stories of Hope* purchased at full price, CWR will donate an additional copy to a prisoner. Or, you can buy a box of 20 copies to donate to a prison in need. For more information, visit **www.cwr.org.uk/hope**

It is CWR's privilege to be able to send resources and daily Bible reading notes into prisons in the UK and around the world, not just at Easter...

'All these years I was searching for something when God was there all along, I just needed to open my ears and heart to let Him in and show me. Thank you again for your wisdom, blessing and light during this time.' Prisoner, HMP

To find out more about CWR's prison ministry, visit **www.cwr.org/prisons**

How do you pray?

FOR READING & MEDITATION – ROMANS 11:25–36

*'Oh, the depth of the riches of the wisdom and knowledge of God!
How unsearchable his judgments' (v33)*

We are reflecting on the truth that because of the common origin of our creation and our redemption, an examination of our lateral relationships will help in an examination of our vertical relationships – and vice versa. In the light of this, permit me to ask you once again: what is your prayer life like? Perhaps you do not pray at all – or very little. Are you like the little boy who, when his vicar asked him if he prayed every day, replied, 'No – because there are some days when I don't need anything'? Or are you like the man who said, 'I pray only in an advisory capacity'?

FURTHER STUDY

Psa. 148; 149; 150

1. Pray these Psalms out loud.

2. How do you feel now?

If you do pray, how do you pray? Sadly, many people view prayer only as a means of asking God for the things they lack. That is one aspect of prayer, but not the whole part. There is an aspect of true connected prayer that involves the cultivation of an intimate relationship with Jesus.

If I were to tiptoe into your home one day and overhear you praying, would I hear prayers that are dutiful but riddled with clichés? Would I hear passion in your prayers, spontaneous praise, expressions of thankfulness to God for His everlasting love and mercy, joy, surprise and laughter at having been chosen by Him to bear His name? I have selected today's reading to highlight how the apostle, in the midst of writing some very taxing theology, allows his heart to overflow to God in a delightful doxology. Hear the passion that pours from his heart as he breaks out: 'Oh, the depth of the riches of God's wisdom and knowledge'. He can hardly contain his feelings. If only our prayer life could be more like that – punctuated by spontaneous outbursts of affection and praise.

Father, forgive me if my prayer life fails to function on an intimate level. Deliver me from mere dutiful praying. Set my soul on fire with love for You so that affection rises because it must. In Jesus' name. Amen.

A lapsed love

FOR READING & MEDITATION – REVELATION 2:1–7

'Yet I hold this against you: You have forsaken your first love.' (v4)

Yesterday we ended by longing for our prayer life to have more spontaneity, affection and praise. Have you ever (or do you ever) tell Jesus how much you love Him when you pray? If our prayer life is simply filled with clichés, and an intimacy with our creator and redeemer is absent, then it is time to pause and ask ourselves whether we have become too familiar with the wonder of God's love, mercy and His amazing grace.

When we first encounter God's saving love, either through a sudden dramatic conversion or coming to faith more gradually, we are often so overwhelmed by the truth that our souls have been touched by the Ageless Romancer that we experience an intensity comparable to falling in love. But it is not unusual to find that passion beginning to diminish as time goes on. What we experienced as earth-shaking and soul-changing is later taken for granted. The freshness of our spiritual experience becomes stale. In the words of today's verse, we have 'forsaken our first love'. We preserve the importance of our conversion by regularly attending church, reading the Bible, praying, celebrating communion; but the intimate, passionate feelings we once had for Jesus are no longer there.

FURTHER STUDY

Jer. 2:1–8;
Matt. 6:1–15;
23:1–28

1. What are the indications that love has lapsed?

2. What is the remedy?

When this happens, it is not unusual for Christians to compensate for the loss of these loving feelings by throwing themselves into endless Christian activities – more committee meetings, more spiritual projects, and so on. But ceaseless rounds of Christian activity are but the ashes upon a rusty altar if we lack a blazing passionate love for Jesus Christ. It's a sad time in our Christian experience when orthodoxy is preserved but intimacy is lost.

Father, help me to see if I am compensating for a lapsed love by throwing myself more energetically into Christian activity. If passion and intimacy is dying, then I ask You in Your mercy to forgive me and restore me. In Jesus' name. Amen.

Put your soul on alert

FOR READING & MEDITATION – REVELATION 1:1–8

*'To him who loves us and has freed us from our sins by his blood…
be glory and power for ever and ever!' (vv5–6)*

We read yesterday how the church in Ephesus was very active, but Jesus knew that they had left their first love. More than anything, Jesus looked for their love. Lacking that, they possibly lacked everything.

How different was the apostle who conveyed Jesus' concerns to the Ephesian church. He is not afraid to use intimate, passionate expressions, because that is the way he felt about Jesus. I say again, it is in our personal and private prayer life that we can best notice whether or not our intimate connectedness with Jesus has dissipated. When prayer, the most personal aspect of the spiritual life, becomes riddled with clichés and there is no love and tender intimacy running through our conversations with the Saviour, then it's time to put our souls on alert. It is a sure sign that the fires of passion and intimacy are beginning to get low.

Eugene Peterson says, 'One of the most challenging tasks of those who are called to shepherd the flock of God is helping them stay alert to the magnificence of their salvation.' When I was a pastor, I found that I could hear by the way people prayed whether their relationship with Jesus was beginning to wane. When that happened, I would ask (at an appropriate moment) something like this: 'How are things between you and Jesus? Are you in love with Jesus as much as you used to be?' If the answer was not particularly positive, I would gently enquire some more. There is always a reason for a lapse in one's feelings for our heavenly Father. It might seem that love dies of its own accord. But it only seems like that. When love wanes, there is a reason.

FURTHER STUDY

Luke 18:9–14;
Eph. 1

1. Compare the prayer attitudes of the Pharisee and the tax collector.

2. What emotions does Paul express about God?

Father, I need insight and understanding to know why my love for You can lapse and wane. Give me that insight and understanding, I pray. I want to think love, act love and feel love for You – always. In Jesus' name. Amen.

Easter – only once a year?

FOR READING & MEDITATION – 1 CORINTHIANS 15:1–14

'that he was buried, that he was raised on the third day according to the Scriptures' (v4)

We continue reflecting on how it is so easy to allow our passionate, intimate love for Jesus to wane. Many pastors will tell you that one of the greatest challenges they have is to move people beyond religious rituals toward personal love for Jesus. Many stop at the rituals – Communion, public reading of the Scriptures, the liturgy, holy festival days, such as Easter, and so on – and somehow fail to move on to a warm, personal, intimate relationship with the living Saviour.

It is not difficult, as many pastors know, to fill a church around Easter time and focus a congregation on the resurrection of Christ. But, as the principal of the college where I trained for the ministry used to say: 'Your task as preachers is to gather people every Sunday and to nurture their participation in the resurrection life of Christ that works just as well at nine o'clock on any Monday morning as at any Easter Sunday sunrise service.'

The Christian writer Ian Macpherson highlights that the first apostles did not so much preach about the resurrection of Christ, but about Christ and the resurrection. It was Christ first, the event second.

FURTHER STUDY

Jer. 31:31–34;
John 14:16–17;
Rom. 8:9–11;
Gal. 2:20;
Col. 1:9–27

1. How is Christ in you?

2. Why is Christ in you?

How is it with you? Is the resurrection of Jesus something you only celebrate once a year? Or do you daily feel an inner flame as you reflect on the truth that Christ is not just alive, but alive *in you*? In a couple of weeks' time, millions will gather in churches to join in the celebrations of Easter but, sadly, many of them will stop at the institutional and never get to the personal; they will be more taken up with the event than the risen Jesus who stands behind it all. Let's ask ourselves: do we celebrate Easter every day?

My Father and my God, help me to draw on the life and strength of the living Lord Jesus within me every day. Forgive me if I live some other way. Amen.

The vocabulary of love

FOR READING & MEDITATION – EXODUS 15:1–21

'Sing to the LORD, for he is highly exalted. The horse and its rider he has hurled into the sea.' (v21)

Most Christians, myself included, will confess that it is not always easy to stay 'alert to the magnificence of salvation'. As one writer put it: 'When we first engage with God's saving love, our hearts are overwhelmed – but after a while, it becomes a familiar part of the landscape, one religious item among many others… the vocabulary of salvation is reduced to the level of a Valentine-card verse.' How do we protect ourselves from losing touch with this vibrant aspect of our relationship with Jesus?

FURTHER STUDY

Psa. 116–118;
Matt. 26:17–30;
1 Cor. 5:7–8;
11:23–32

1. In what way does the Passover speak of Christ?

2. How do the Psalms contain the vocabulary of love and sacrifice?

Here we may be helped by considering how our Jewish friends guard against the Passover becoming mere ritual. The Jewish Passover celebrates the Exodus from Egypt, which is one of the most awesome and majestic movements of God in the Old Testament. The event has been kept alive by the Passover, and retelling the story again and again. At some point in Jewish history, the leaders in Israel realised that the Exodus story, marvellous and magnificent as it was, could with constant retelling become stale, and nothing more than a religious ritual.

To protect against this danger they introduced into the Passover celebrations the reading of the Song of Songs, that passionate and tender love story composed by King Solomon. The leaders hoped that, by ending the meal with the Song of Songs, they would draw the attention of the participants to inward relationships. They believed that by entering into the vocabulary of the Song of Songs – the vocabulary of love – the participating families would think not merely in terms of action, but of romance also. Perhaps a few days meditating on the Song of Songs will help us too.

Father, forgive me if I think only of my relationship with You in terms of action and not romance. May my longing to have a deeper loving relationship with You be matched by that vocabulary of love. In Jesus' name. Amen.

The holy of holies

FOR READING & MEDITATION – 1 KINGS 4:29–34

'Men of all nations came to listen to Solomon's wisdom, sent by all the kings of the world, who had heard of his wisdom.' (v34)

Yesterday we said that entering into the vocabulary of the Song of Songs, the vocabulary of love and intimacy, might enable us to think about our salvation not merely in terms of action but of romance. Whenever I have felt the fire of love for Jesus begin to die down, I have soaked myself in the Song of Songs.

The Welsh preacher Christmas Evans said of the Song of Songs: 'If the embers of love for Jesus are growing cold in your life, read the Song of Solomon; its breath will cause the dying embers to burst again into flame.' Eugene Peterson says: 'The lyrics of the Song of Songs are a guard against every tendency to turn living faith into a lifeless religion; it is the most inward of all the books of the Bible.' Rabbi Akiba, a Jewish commentator, said of it: 'all the world is not as worthy as the day on which the Song of Songs was given to Israel. For all the writings are holy, but the Song of Songs is the holy of holies.' All the intimacies possible to men and women in courtship and in marriage are contained in this book, and are an index to the delights and difficulties in our loving response to the God who loves us.

Don't be put off by the metaphors used in the Song of Songs, for as Philip Rieff says, '[sex] and religion are intricately interwoven, they deal with the basic elements of intimacy and the stuff of ecstasy'. And though the word 'God' is not mentioned even once, the book helps us understand how to develop a life of intimacy with Him. If nothing is more important than maintaining a life of romance with God, then how thankful we ought to be that God has included this book in the Bible!

FURTHER STUDY

Heb. 9:1–10:25

1. What is meant by the term 'holy of holies'?

2. Who is allowed into the holy of holies?

Father, I am keen to develop a more intimate relationship with You. As I acquaint myself yet again with the passionate words of the Song of Songs, may greater passion get hold of me. In Jesus' name I ask it. Amen.

'Kiss me'

FOR READING & MEDITATION – SONG OF SONGS 1:1–2

'Let him kiss me with the kisses of his mouth' (v2)

Yesterday we said that one of the best ways of maintaining a sense of romance in our relationship with Jesus is to soak ourselves in the Song of Songs. There are three themes running through the Song of Songs: love's yearning, love's difficulties and love's response – and all three are touched upon in the first 11 verses. Let's look briefly at these three themes in order for us to familiarise ourselves with its romantic and intimate language, and hopefully deepen and enrich our own relationship with Jesus Christ.

FURTHER STUDY

Gen. 32:1–33:12;
Luke 15:11–24

1. How did Esau kiss the soul of Jacob?

2. How did the father kiss the soul of the prodigal?

The book is a love poem in which two people in love share their thoughts and feelings about one another and with one another. The NIV refers to the man as the 'Lover' and to the woman as the 'Beloved'. The Lover is obviously absent. The first words in the Song are, 'Let him kiss me with the kisses of his mouth'. *The Message* renders it, 'Kiss me – full on the mouth' – not just a kiss on the cheek. It is a direct and passionate appeal for closeness and intimacy.

The speaker is not interested in talking about love or merely conversing about it with her friends, but longs for the touch of her lover's lips upon hers. 'Intimacy', says one philosopher, 'is a requirement of wholeness; life to be meaningful must be joined'. How true this is in the realm of the soul as well as the physical. I can tell you I have heard a comparable cry to 'Kiss me' coming from the hearts of many in the counselling room. The soul, you see, often longs to be kissed as much as the lips do. What we all long for deep down is to be known and loved – and loved intimately. Where love is absent, the soul will for ever remain dissatisfied.

Jesus, lover of my soul, help me see that the longings of my heart are not for prestige, or power, but passion. I am made for Your intimate love. Help me be open to that love, for without it my soul withers and dies. Amen.

Satisfied yet unsatisfied

FOR READING & MEDITATION – JOHN 4:1–26

'Everyone who drinks this water will be thirsty again, but whoever drinks the water I give him will never thirst.' (v13)

We spend another day reflecting on the thought that we touched on yesterday, namely that the soul longs to be kissed as much as the lips. Counsellors are trained to hear, in a spiritual sense, the inarticulate cry, 'Kiss me'. It is hidden there under all kinds of demands and requests. Let me share with you something that I have learned over the years: one of the reasons why obsessions and compulsions arise in us is because the soul does not experience deeply enough the satisfaction that comes from a passionate and intimate relationship with Jesus. I will go further and say this: to the degree that the soul does not allow itself to be overwhelmed by divine love, to that degree it will experience problems.

The following statement by George Macdonald took my breath away when I first encountered it: 'When a man knocks at the door of a brothel, what he is really looking for is God.' I said to myself, 'Whatever does he mean?' Then the light came on: deep down in our hearts all of us long for a relationship with God, the Ageless Romancer, and if we do not find that love, then we will search for a substitute. Sex might be passionate and momentarily satisfying, but it is short-lived. The soul longs for something deeper than that – what I have heard described as 'the divine romance'.

Those who open their souls to the love of God in Christ find that the satisfaction He gives makes all other demands less clamorous. Once we know Jesus, however, and our hearts are filled with His love, though we are satisfied we long for more. 'Kiss me' is always the cry of the soul that has been set on fire with God's love.

FURTHER STUDY

Gen. 27:1–29;
Eccl. 1:8; 4:8;
5:10; 6:7;
Prov. 27:20

1. Why did Isaac want to be kissed?

2. What is the experience of men without God?

Lord Jesus Christ, I have experienced Your love and my heart longs for more. The lips of my soul yearn to feel the impact of Your loving touch. Touch me once more today. In Jesus' name. Amen.

Better than wine

FOR READING & MEDITATION – SONG OF SONGS 1:2

'for your love is more delightful than wine.' (v2)

The woman in the Song of Songs is clear as to why she wants to be kissed on the mouth. Here is her explanation: 'for your love is more delightful than wine.' Kisses on the mouth indicate closeness, intimacy and passion.

Here in the United Kingdom, football (soccer) is one of our passions. When a goal is scored in an important match, the team members hug and kiss the goal scorer all over his face. Those who give lingering kisses mouth to mouth tend to be lovers. But in what sense is love better than wine? The reference to wine in this context has to do with conviviality. Leaving aside the pros and cons of wine-drinking for the moment, the thought here is that, just as wine relaxes inhibitions, stimulates conversation, bridges the chasms that sometimes separate one person from another, love also accomplishes the same thing – only better. As one commentator expresses it: 'It joins the "Thou" and the "I", dissolves the separating wall and engenders the communication of emotion, thought and purpose.' Is not one of the reasons why we became Christians because we tried the 'wine' of the world and were dissatisfied with it? It worked for a while, but what our souls long for is something that will satisfy eternally.

FURTHER STUDY

Psa. 104:14–15;
Matt. 9:15–17;
John 2:1–11;
Eph. 5:18–19

1. Why did God give us wine?
2. What is the new wine?

One of the tragedies in many churches is that people come in having rejected the pseudo-intimacies of the world for the intimacies of salvation, and immediately they are pounced upon to become involved in a community project or join a committee. First steps in discipleship are about learning that the main purpose of the Christian life is developing an intimate, passionate relationship with Jesus.

Father, forgive us when we seem to be more concerned with turning Your sheep into workers before helping them to develop an intimate relationship with You. Forgive us and help us put first things first. In Jesus' name. Amen.

Names – the stuff of intimacy

MON
19 MAR

FOR READING & MEDITATION – SONG OF SONGS 1:3

'Pleasing is the fragrance of your perfumes; your name is like perfume poured out.' (v3)

The Beloved continues her reverie by reflecting on the fact that the name of her Lover affected her ears in the same way that a fragrant perfume affected her nostrils. I have heard it said, 'Intimacy is not a vague mystic merging into the world of the soul; it is personal and particular joining with a specific other: Adam with Eve, Solomon with the Shulamite woman.' Everyone has a name; it personalises. This is one reason the Bible places importance on names; they give historical, concrete meaning to God's story. Names are the stuff of intimacy. 'The church roll', I was told when training for the ministry, 'is one of the most important things in the house of God.'

When I was a pastor, I regularly used to take the church roll and pray for the members of that church by name – ten a day. Without names, there could be no effective pastoral work. In his book *I Am an Impure Thinker*, Rosenstock-Huessy says: 'As long as we are only taught and addressed in the mass, our name never falls upon us as the power that dresses wounds, lifts our hearts, and makes us rise up and walk.' Just as the Shulamite woman in the Song of Songs delighted at the sound of her Lover's name, so do we who are Christians rejoice in the name of our Saviour Jesus.

It was said of the American revivalist Jonathan Edwards that though he was a stern and somewhat austere man, whenever anyone mentioned to him the name of Jesus, his whole demeanour would light up with pure joy. How infinitely precious to those who love the Saviour is His name. As the old hymn puts it, 'it soothes our sorrows, heals our wounds and drives away our fear'.

FURTHER STUDY

Exod. 28:1–30;
Isa. 9:6–7;
Matt. 1:18–23;
Acts 3:1–4:12

1. How did the high priest approach God?
2. What is special about the name(s) of Jesus?

Jesus, 'Your name is as ointment poured forth'. How much it means to me – salvation, healing, deliverance, freedom, abundant joy – all these and ten thousand more. I am forever grateful. Amen.

Let what you leave behind be the fruit of what you sowed

Death brings life, Jesus taught, just as the grain of wheat multiplies its fruitfulness when it dies (John 12:24).

Selwyn Hughes, CWR founder and creator of *Every Day with Jesus* asked, 'Why would you need a stack of notes in heaven?' He spoke of investing money in God's kingdom, 'because that is where we will be spending eternity.'

Let what you leave be the fruit of what you sowed during your life.

'tell to the coming generation the glorious deeds of the LORD, and his might, and the wonders that he has done.' – Psalm 78:4

What will your legacy be?

If CWR has impacted your faith, and encouraged you in your life, we would like to invite you to prayerfully consider how leaving a legacy to CWR might be one way in which God multiplies your fruitfulness after He calls you home.

Your gift could help us continue to...
· Help people apply God's Word to their daily lives
· Serve the Church by developing new resources and teaching
· Equip and train counsellors all over the world to help people live their lives to the fullness God intended

After you have made provision for your family, we would advise you to consult with your solicitor or legal advisor regarding leaving a gift in your Will to CWR. If you have already made your Will but would like to leave a gift to CWR, you can easily do so by completing a codicil form.

For further information on legacies please write to us:
CWR, Waverley Abbey House, Waverley Lane, Farnham, Surrey, GU9 8EP.
Tel: **01252 784709** or email: **legacy@cwr.org.uk**

What's in a name?

FOR READING & MEDITATION – PSALM 8:1–9

'O LORD, our Lord, how majestic is your name in all the earth!' (vv1,9)

We spend another day reflecting on the power of a name. Shakespeare coined the phrase, 'What's in a name?' Everything. If we mention John Wesley, Martin Luther, Winston Churchill, we know at once what to expect. Their names stand for something and communicate a clear message. How supremely is this so when we talk about Jesus! The Beloved in the Song of Songs says her Lover's name was like a perfume poured out. Even the costliest perfume is scentless when sealed up.

FURTHER STUDY

Mark 14:1–3;
Luke 7:36–50;
2 Cor. 2:14–16;
Eph. 5:2

1. What is necessary before fragrance is released?

2. What is 'the perfume of Jesus'?

The late Lindsay Glegg, a British preacher, told of a department store in London where on hot summer days, before air conditioning, shoppers were sprayed as they entered with a fine invisible jet of perfume. Many used to wonder at the pleasant odour that permeated the store, but the real reason was not discovered for years. There comes to mind the words of a beautiful hymn that used to be sung a long time ago:

My Lord has garments so wondrous fine,
And myrrh their texture fills;
Its fragrance reaches to this heart of mine,
With joy my being thrills.
Out of the ivory palaces, into a world of woe,
Only His great eternal love
Made my Saviour go.

The apostle Paul wrote of 'the aroma of Christ' (2 Cor. 2:15). Are we permeated by that invisible aroma of heaven that He brought to this stifling valley of tears? And are we letting that fragrance linger on those we rub shoulders with? Truly fragrant is the name of our wonderful Saviour, Jesus.

Lord Jesus, the more I think about what You mean to me the more my heart is turned to joy. For all Your goodness and worth, and the life You bring to my soul, I offer You my thanks, my praise and my life. Amen.

Let's run off together

'Take me away with you – let us hurry! The king has brought me into his chambers.' (v4)

The maidens referred to in this passage are considered by commentators to be unmarried friends of the absent Lover. Everyone, it seemed, had eyes for the Beloved's Lover. It was no wonder to her that everyone loved to say his name! 'Take me away with you!' she continues. 'Let's run off together!... We'll celebrate, we'll sing, we'll make great music. Yes! For your love is better than vintage wine' (*The Message*). Clearly, the woman imagines herself to be ensconced in the apartment of her royal Lover. Is there anything that anyone desires more than to be with the one who is loved? Permit me to ask you a personal question: how deeply do you desire to deepen your relationship with Jesus? Did you rise this morning to look into His face, your first thoughts towards Jesus asking Him to stay close, to take your hand as you walk out together into the day?

'There are two evidences of growing in grace and in the knowledge of our Lord Jesus Christ,' said Harold Horton, author and preacher. 'We long to be with our Lord through prayer and the reading of His Word, and we are quick to pick up our feet and run the way of His commandments.' Loving Jesus is not just telling Him, but also following and obeying Him.

There are those who enter into enthusiastic times of devotion and who tell Jesus they love Him, but their walk is not consistent with their talk. Then there are those who obey His commandments, but who feel uncomfortable when it comes to telling Him how much they love Him. Both are important. We show that we love Him by the way we walk before Him, but I think He likes to hear us say it too.

FURTHER STUDY

1 Chron. 29:10–20;
1 John 2:1–11;
3:1–24

1. How did David link petition and praise in prayer?

2. How does John combine talk and walk?

Jesus, I'm sorry for the times when my prayer life is mainly requests and petitions, with little expression of personal passion or praise. I love You, Jesus, take my hand as we walk out into the day. I ask this in Your name. Amen.

My glorious dress

FOR READING & MEDITATION – SONG OF SONGS 1:5–6

*'Dark am I, yet lovely, O daughters of Jerusalem,
dark like the tents of Kedar' (v5)*

Having looked at the verses that spell out the yearning of the Beloved for the Lover, we come now to consider another theme that runs through the Song of Songs – love's difficulties. In this passage, the joys of anticipating spending time with her Lover seem to give way to questioning her own desirability. For a moment it looks as if fearful feelings about her own unworthiness are going to inhibit her longings and desires for love.

Addressing the daughters of Jerusalem (the girls who helped prepare for her marriage), she is concerned about her unattractiveness. 'I am... Weather-darkened like Kedar desert tents,' she says (*The Message*). It seems that she had worked in the early part of her life in the vineyards. She seeks to reassure herself, however, that though she is weathered she is still elegant. 'Dark am I, yet lovely.'

FURTHER STUDY

1 Sam. 9:15–21;
Matt. 3:1–15;
11:7–11

1. How did Saul and John see themselves?

2. How did the Lord see them?

How many Christians, I wonder, live their lives burdened with the thought that they are unworthy of God's love? If this is you, reflect on these words of P.T. Forsyth: 'No one is worthy of divine love. It was our misery, not our merit, that acted as a magnet to draw the Almighty toward us. Rejoice in the fact that though you were not worthy, you have been made worthy through the righteousness that Jesus offers us through His Cross.' I think the lines of a hymn put it more eloquently and beautifully than I ever could:

*Jesus, Thy blood and righteousness
My beauty are, my glorious dress;
Midst flaming worlds, in these arrayed,
With joy shall I lift up my head.*

Father, my beauty is Jesus. Justified by faith, I stand in Your presence as if I had never sinned, clothed with the glorious robe of His righteousness. Thank You, my Father. Amen.

I belong to my lover

'Do not stare at me because I am dark, because I am darkened by the sun.' (v6)

One of the difficulties we have in responding to the love that reaches down to us from above is that it is so freely given. It seems utterly amazing that we are adopted into the family of God and given the honour of being called His children. But to be called the Beloved, pursued by God Himself, is surely something that takes our breath away. We may be staggered by it, but it is an established biblical truth – you are beloved of God. If God is an Ageless Romancer, the 'Pursuer', then there has to be a Beloved, the Pursued. This is our role in God's story. He has an eternal plan to prepare a Bride (His Church) for Himself.

Deep down in our hearts, all we have ever wanted is to be loved unconditionally, and with a love that guarantees never to withdraw itself. And in God we have that kind of love! 'Love comes from God', John reminds us. We don't have to get God to love us by doing things right. I have met many people who think that they have to love God before He loves them. Consider with me what John has to say about this: 'This is love: not that we loved God, but that he loved us and sent his Son as an atoning sacrifice for our sins' (1 John 4:10).

There is nothing we have to do to keep God loving us, for His love is not based on what we have done or on what we are in ourselves but on who we are in His sight – His Beloved. God has pursued us from farther than space and longer ago than time. Incredible though it is, however, we are to respond in the same way as the Beloved in the Song of Songs: 'I belong to my lover, and his desire is for me' (Songs 7:10).

FURTHER STUDY

Judg. 6:11–24;
Luke 5:1–9;
22:31–62;
John 13:1–9;
21:15–17

1. What did Gideon and Peter think of themselves?

2. What did the Lord think of them?

Thank You, my Father, that in You I've found a love that satisfies my heart and satisfies the deepest thirst of my soul. The sheer power of Your love overcomes all my resistance and distrust. I am grateful more than my words can convey. Amen.

The dark night of the soul

FOR READING & MEDITATION – SONG OF SONGS 1:7

'Tell me, you whom I love, where you graze your flock and where you rest your sheep at midday.' (v7)

Another of love's difficulties is maintaining intimacy. Although God has provided the means for us to keep close to Him (through prayer and Bible meditation), there are times when we experience obstacles. In today's passage, the woman seems not to know where her Lover is, and she is desperate to find him. *The Message* renders the woman's words as: 'Tell me where you're working – I love you so much – Tell me where you're tending your flocks, where you let them rest at noontime. Why should I be the one left out, outside the orbit of your tender care?' The figure of speech has changed from a king (v4) to a shepherd. Many commentators take this to mean that the woman's Lover was a shepherd, while others think it is using a poetic form of expression. The reference to the 'veiled woman' suggests the role of a prostitute (see Gen. 38:14–15) and the woman is really saying, 'I don't want to wander aimlessly looking for you among the shepherds, giving the impression I am a loose woman'. Let's face the fact that, even as Christians, there are times when it seems that Jesus, our Lover, is absent from us.

FURTHER STUDY

Songs 3:1–4; 5:2–6:3; 1 Kings 19:1–21; Psa. 42; 43

1. Describe the emotions of Elijah and David.

2. What were the results of reunion?

Later in the song she has an experience where she cries: 'I looked for him but did not find him. I called him but he did not answer' (Songs 5:6). The old saints called this 'the dark night of the soul', those times when one knows intellectually that God is there but the emotions say He is absent. No one has an adequate explanation for this, except that if there is no sin in one's life, then the absence is for our good – and the reunion when we experience it will be all the more joyful. The thirsts God creates in us lead to the satisfactions He promised.

Father, whenever I perceive a lack of Your intimate touch on my life, help me understand that this does not mean Your love is changeable. Show me how to let it spur me to a deeper knowledge of You and Your ways. In Jesus' name. Amen.

The mystery of absence

FOR READING & MEDITATION – SONG OF SONGS 1:8

*'If you do not know, most beautiful of women,
follow the tracks of the sheep' (v8)*

The Lord's 'most beautiful' and holiest children can miss the steps He has taken – not necessarily through sin, but through what the saints of a previous generation referred to as 'the mystery of His absence'. For no reason discoverable to us, He may leave the familiar path on which together we were walking. If that is your experience right now, remember that God is sovereign. He leads where He will, and wherever He leads is right. Remember too, when He leaves us feeling confused, wondering which way He has gone, that He is leading still. His absence will urge us to cry: 'Tell me, you whom I love, where you graze your flock'.

The answer given to the woman by her Lover is, 'follow the tracks of the sheep'. To find the shepherd, follow the tracks of the faithful sheep. Multitudes throughout time have testified that, when they have lost track of the shepherd, they have found Him again by following the track worn and created by the holy feet of the faithful people of God.

Walking where the saints have walked is important. The hymn writer expressed it well:

> *They marked the footsteps that he trod,*
> *His zeal inspired their breast,*
> *And following their incarnate God,*
> *Possessed the promised rest.*

Others have gone the way we have; let us rejoice and follow them. If we are walking where the saints have walked, the path will lead us safely to the shepherd and fresh pastures.

FURTHER STUDY

Heb. 11:1–13; 13:7;
1 Pet. 2:21

1. Who is your favourite Bible character, and why?

2. Who do we ultimately follow, and how?

God my Father, help me learn this lesson, that whenever I feel that You are absent, to follow the tracks worn by the feet of the people of God. Show me how to tread 'where the saints have trod'. In Jesus' name. Amen.

When all comparisons fail

FOR READING & MEDITATION – SONG OF SONGS 1:9

'I liken you, my darling, to a mare harnessed to one of the chariots of Pharaoh.' (v9)

I commented earlier that three themes dominate the Song of Songs: love's yearning, love's difficulties and love's response. Observing that all three themes are present in the first 11 verses of the book, we have explored love's yearning (vv1–4), love's difficulties (vv5–7) and we now come to love's response. How ready the Lover is to speak encouraging words of praise to his Beloved. What sweet comparisons he uses to delight her heart.

FURTHER STUDY

Deut. 32:9–14;
Zech. 2:8;
Isa. 43:1–21;
1 John 3:16;
4:7–16

1. Who is the apple of God's eye?

2. To what extent does God love us?

King Solomon was well known for his love of horses. We read in 1 Kings 10:26–29 that he had 1,400 chariots and 12,000 horses. The passage tells us also that on one occasion, Solomon paid 150 shekels for a horse that he imported from Egypt. But it was not with that horse that he compares the Beloved; it was with a mare harnessed to one of the chariots of Pharaoh. As one of Pharaoh's chariot steeds made all the other excellent horses seem commonplace, so his Beloved's excelling beauty made all other beautiful women ordinary.

It has been said by one commentator that this flattering comparison is similar to Theocritus's praise of the beautiful Helen of Troy. If you are familiar with the story, you will know that when she was taken to Troy by Paris, her husband Menelaus, King of Greece, amassed a great army and set off with a thousand ships to lay siege on Troy and win Helen back. Few have ever been so pursued. She must have known beyond all doubt that she mattered. It is the same with us, God's redeemed ones. We mean more to Him than anything in the whole world. We are His Beloved. No language is able, and no comparisons possible, to explain how fully and how deeply we are loved.

Father, the fact that I matter to You fills me with ever increasing wonder. How can it be? Help me not to dwell on how unworthy I might feel, but receive and enjoy Your love. In Jesus' name. Amen.

Gifts and graces

'Your cheeks are beautiful with ear-rings, your neck with strings of jewels.' (v10)

How beautiful the Beloved must have looked with the gifts of her Lover upon her head and neck. What the Lover extravagantly bestows, He has a right to extravagantly praise. The beauty of our Lord's Beloved (you and me) is not so much in ourselves, our 'cheeks' or 'neck', but in what He provides freely to us. It is His gifts and graces that make us what we are. There is nothing shoddy about the heavenly provision of gifts: all precious metal and flawless stones, shining bright and pure.

One of the hymns I used to enjoy, simply for its poetic beauty, spoke of being garmented by the grace of God. After I became a Christian, knowing through experience what the hymnist was trying to convey, it had a much greater meaning for me. One of the verses said this:

> *In Calvary's fount Thou washed us, whose hands were red with blood*
> *Thy holy oil anointeth us, with broidered work of God,*
> *And linen fine Thou girdest us, with strength our feet are shod.*
> *How wonderful our heritage, had we but eyes to see,*
> *Yet all we are and have and claim cometh in grace from Thee*
> *Our hearts hold naught but nothingness – and Thy sufficiency.*

The world obsesses after outward embellishments, but the Beloved delights in the developing of a meek and quiet spirit, modest sincerity, godly trust, sincere service, and happy gratitude – the gifts of grace.

FURTHER STUDY

Songs 4:1–17;
Isa. 61:1–11;
1 Pet. 3:1–7;
Rev. 21:1–24

1. What does jewellery speak of?

2. What are true spiritual jewels?

Father, what wondrous changes You have provided for me through Your grace. Truly, all I have and claim, come in grace from You. Open my eyes to see even more clearly the transformation You have made in my life. In Jesus' name. Amen.

From here to eternity

FOR READING & MEDITATION – SONG OF SONGS 1:11

'We will make you ear-rings of gold, studded with silver.' (v11)

The Lover's gifts make the Beloved beautiful and lovely today, but the Lover's promise is to make her even more beautiful in the future: 'I'm making jewelry for you, gold and silver jewelry that will mark and accent your beauty' (*The Message*). Jesus, who through His own personal sacrifice offers and gives us His gifts and graces, makes us attractive in the present – but to these things He will one day add even more gifts of beauty. As Harold Horton expressed it: 'Gold to the gold of divine graces, silver to the silver of redemption's glories, jewels to the jewels of personal excellencies... superlative loveliness exceeding our wildest imagination is His blessed plan for us.'

FURTHER STUDY

Isa. 62:1–12;
Eph. 5:22–32;
Rev. 19:1–9

1. What is your concept of the bride of Christ?

2. Do you usually think of yourself as a 'sheep' or a 'bride'?

Whatever beauty we have now is nothing compared to the beauty that awaits us when we, the bride of Christ, shall be clothed in heaven's finest, ready for the marriage to our heavenly Bridegroom. I know the bridal imagery often fails to capture a man's heart, but I encourage male readers to think of it in terms of the highest intimacy possible. He who has won our hearts through the cross, and who has wooed us by His Spirit, will one day wed us. The marriage metaphor is used to reveal to us that our Lover's intention is to be united with us in the most intimate way for all eternity.

Though the words that follow were spoken to the nation of Israel they apply also to Christ's Church: 'As a young man marries a maiden, so will your sons marry you; as a bridegroom rejoices over his bride, so will your God rejoice over you' (Isa. 62:5). Such is our Lord's delight in us. Our Lover delights in us enough to make us His own for all eternity.

My Father and my God, it would be enough to be in heaven but to be united with Christ for all eternity exceeds my highest expectations. Nothing is more wonderful on earth or in heaven. I am humbled, yet grateful. Thank You, my Father. Amen.

An act of genius

FOR READING & MEDITATION – SONG OF SONGS 1:12–14

'My lover is to me a cluster of henna blossoms from the vineyards of En Gedi.' (v14)

I introduced this section on the Song of Songs by drawing your attention to the fact that the Jews, to protect themselves from engaging in just a ritual, ended the Passover meal (the Seder) with reading the Song of Songs. It is difficult to trace the name of the leaders who introduced this assignment into the feast but for me it was clearly an act of spiritual genius.

'The reading of the Song in the context of Passover,' says one commentator, 'is a demonstration that the glorious, once-for-all historical event of salvation, in which God's people are established in the way of God's love, is workable in the everyday domestic settings of intimacy between persons. It bridges the transition from the Exodus event to daily activities so that there is no loss of wonder, intensity or joy.'

Not only did Jesus come to rescue us from the slavery of sin – which is commemorated in the meal that He instituted at the Last Supper – but our study of the Song of Songs shows that aspect of our salvation where the Heavenly Lover came to woo us as His beloved bride, and longs for us to have a deep, ongoing relationship with Him. It begins, as we saw, with a yearning to be kissed, and ends with a longing for even deeper intimacy. After Easter, we will turn to consider other aspects of God's passionate love for His people. My prayer is that the few days we have spent exploring the first 11 verses will help realign any leanings we might have within us to reduce the faith we experience to a tradition. The story of the Exodus linked to the Song of Songs reinforces the truth that God saves us – His people – because He loves us. *Passionately!*

FURTHER STUDY

Songs 4:8–5:1; 6:2–8:10

1. What are your main impressions of Solomon's Song?

2. Meditate on Song of Songs 7:1.

Father, there is in my heart a deep longing for intimacy, for beauty, for adventure. The intimacy I enjoy with You now is just a taste of what is to come. I get the taste now; the banquet comes later. Blessed be Your name for ever. Amen.

You supply the willingness

FOR READING & MEDITATION – 1 CORINTHIANS 1:18–25

*'For the message of the cross... to us who are being saved...
is the power of God.' (v18)*

We come once more to Good Friday, the day on which we celebrate how God showed His extreme love for us by sending His only Son Jesus to die for our sins.

Perhaps I have been talking in recent days to someone whose heart has grown cold to the pursuing of the Heavenly Lover; perhaps because other affections have captivated you, and you are finding it difficult to give them up. If that is so, I invite you to stand with me at the cross. There is a strength and power that flows from the cross that can break every bondage and set you free to love your soul's true Lover.

FURTHER STUDY

Isa. 53;
Col. 2:6–3:10

1. What has the cross done?

2. What can the cross still do?

I remember one particular Good Friday when a man came to me before the usual Communion service and said: 'I want to enter into the service, but I will not be taking Communion.' When I asked why, he said: 'I have allowed other affections to take over my heart and I think it would be hypocritical to pretend that Christ means all to me when He only occupies half my heart.' I commended him for his honesty and I urged him to take his confession to God, repent of it and receive God's forgiveness and restoration. The reply he gave was typical of those whose hearts have been distracted by other 'lovers': 'I can't seem to do anything about it. Its power over me is too strong.' He reckoned of course without the power of the cross. I told him: 'You supply the willingness, God will supply the power.'

Later in the service I saw him take Communion, and afterwards I asked him what had happened. He said, 'As you led the meditations on the cross I simply said, "I am willing". Miraculously, the chains dropped away from my heart and my love for the Lord seemed to flame forth once again.' The cross had done it. It always does.

Lord, as once again we contemplate Your sufferings for us, I give you all my heart. Here is my willingness; please supply the power. By the power of Your cross, save me and restore me. In Jesus' name. Amen.

Design your own course

Tailor-made teaching at your own small group venue

Create a relaxed and inspiring teaching session by combining the experience of course leader Andy Peck and the familiar surroundings of your own venue choice. Topics include:

- Strategy
- Leadership
- Mechanics
- Dynamics
- Spiritual life

'The teaching re-energised us, both as individuals and as a group'

We Can Come To You

You can have CWR's teaching brought to your church or small group. Visit **www.cwr.org.uk/wecancometoyou** to find out more.

PICK YOUR COURSE OR SEMINAR

Christ Empowered Living

This foundational day course introduces God's original design for our personalities and how we can live well and deepen our dependence on God.

Seven Laws for Life

This dynamic three-hour seminar considers the seven key elements of a successful Christian life.

The Bible in Two Hours

Your team or small group will enjoy an eye-opening overview of the Bible, which serves as a great foundation to Bible reading.

Inspiring Women · Being a Secure Woman – in an Insecure World

This day, half-day or one-hour seminar unfolds the principles of becoming a secure woman in God – whatever your stage of life or circumstances.

Inspiring Women · Women Mentoring Women

This half-day or one-hour seminar looks at areas of ministry, work and homelife where the influence of godly women can greatly help others.

Inspiring Women · Designed for Living

This one-day seminar looks at how to deepen our dependence on God, resolve personal problems and satisfy our deepest longings.

'So many who were there have let me know how inspired, touched and encouraged they felt... Thank you!'

TAILOR-MADE TEACHING

We offer tailor-made training for leaders of churches and small groups, and for anyone in Church.
Topics include:

- Refreshing your spiritual life
- Helping Christians grow
- Pastoral care
- Preaching
- Leading
- Evangelism
- Coaching
- Discovering your spiritual gifts
- Hearing from God

Why not get in touch today and discuss your requirements?
Call **(+44) 01252 784719**
or email **courses@cwr.org.uk**

HIGHER EDUCATION PROGRAMMES
AT WAVERLEY ABBEY COLLEGE

WAVERLEY ABBEY
COLLEGE

BA (Hons) Counselling*
(4/5 years part-time)

· Equips students for a career in counselling by working towards professional accreditation with a professional body.**

MA Therapeutic Counselling and Psychotherapy*
(2/3 years part-time)

· Designed for qualified therapists
· Developed to broaden skills and expertise in a number of specialist areas.

Certificate/Diploma in Counselling Supervision
(8 blocks of 2-day teaching)

· Equips students with the skills, knowledge and professional development to enable them to provide supervisory support and guidance to counsellors in clinical practice.

MA Counselling
(2/3 years part-time)

· Offers study at a postgraduate level
· Designed for those with a first degree (in any subject) and a Certificate in counselling who wish to train for a professional counselling qualification.**

QAA Reviewed
Quality Assurance Agency
for Higher Education

In partnership with
**Middlesex
University**
London

*These programmes are quality assured by Middlesex University and you will receive a Middlesex award on successful completion.

**Awarding accredited status is at the discretion of the professional body.

Visit www.waverleyabbeycollege.ac.uk or call **01252 784731** or email **registry@waverleyabbeycollege.ac.uk**

The bitter made sweet

FOR READING & MEDITATION – EXODUS 15:22–27

*'the LORD showed him a piece of wood. He threw it into the water,
and the water became sweet.' (v25)*

We pause between Good Friday and Easter Sunday to focus on this unusual but illuminating incident in Old Testament times. After crossing the Red Sea, the people of Israel moved into the wilderness of Shur, where they searched eagerly for water. Ahead of them, at a place called Marah, they see some shimmering waters. But when they reach the pool, they find the waters are too bitter to drink. Moses cries out to God, whereupon the Almighty shows him a piece of wood, which he is commanded to throw into the bitter waters. The second the wood enters the water, it becomes sweet.

There are many acrid waters in life. Sometimes, as we have said, the way God lets things happen, it seems as if He does not care. In one of his books, Oswald Chambers said that life is more tragic than orderly. The question arises: does God have a good heart? Well, when we come to consider the cross the answer is quite clear. A God who would give Himself for me on a cross has got to be good. The cross removes all doubt about it. Speaking for myself, and I know for countless others, the cross sweetens the bitter waters of life and enables me to drink great draughts of His goodness. When life is bitter, when I find its waters murky and choking, I look to the cross. I mentally throw that sacred wood into their depths. Instantly they become sweet.

I live by the cross. I know of no other place to be safe. The cross gives me the basis for believing that the heart that lies behind the universe is good. I have no hesitation in giving Him my love, for I know through what He did for me on the cross that His heart is good. I don't just think it, I know it.

FURTHER STUDY

Num. 21:5–9;
2 Kings 2:19–22;
4:38–41;
John 3:14–17;
Rom. 5:1–21

1. How can bitterness become sweet?

2. How did God unequivocally prove His love for us?

Father, help me for ever to stay close to Your cross – the one thing by which all bitter waters are made sweet. Here all my doubts are dissolved, all my uncertainties disappear. Thank You for the cross. Amen.

A dangerous day

FOR READING & MEDITATION – JOHN 20:1–18; SONG OF SONGS 8:5–7
'Many waters cannot quench love; rivers cannot wash it away.'
(Songs 8:7)

Today we celebrate together Easter Sunday. Easter Day has been regarded by the saints throughout history as the most wonderful day in the Christian calendar. But it is also a most dangerous day, in the sense that I talked about earlier – of celebrating Easter just once a year. Every day of our lives is a response to our risen Lord. The resurrection life of Jesus works as well in December as it does in April. As we said, it is as effective at nine o'clock on any Monday morning as it is at an Easter sunrise service.

FURTHER STUDY

Exod. 16:4–31;
Luke 9:23;
Gal. 2:20;
Heb. 3:13

1. What were the purposes of God in supplying manna?

2. What are the daily experiences of a true disciple?

You may wonder why I have turned again to the Song of Songs, and have linked a passage from that book with the well-known account of John's concerning the resurrection. I am doing it for the same reason that our Jewish friends link the celebration of Passover with the reading of the Song of Songs: to ensure that we don't focus merely on the event, but on the meaning behind the event. And what is the meaning behind Easter? It is that God, our Ageless Romancer, has gone through death, the final barrier, in order to win us back to Himself. In his book *Prayer*, Simon Tugwell says: 'Our hope is God's determination to save us. He will not give in.'

He is a determined Lover, this Man of Calvary. He came through what Paul calls 'the last enemy' – death – to enable us to feel His life and His love reverberating in our souls. So don't think today merely in terms of the resurrection of Christ – that is a doctrine; but let us also think of Jesus and His resurrection – that is a dynamic. Let us make sure on this Easter Day that in proclaiming the truth of God, we do not lose touch with the love of God.

Lord Jesus, help Your Church worldwide to see that Easter is a cause for rejoicing – not just once a year, but daily. I live by resurrection life, not just today but every day. I am eternally grateful. Amen.

The habit of a **lifetime**

CWR wants to help people of all ages develop their relationship with God, which is why we enjoy creating relevant, contemporary and engaging daily Bible reading notes to reach every generation.

Having published *All Together* last year, this new family devotional *Time Together* brings parents and children together to enjoy a shared, daily experience of the Bible. This relatable devotional, written by Steve and Bekah Legg, will engage the whole family with God's Word – whether around the kitchen table, or just before bedtime!

And with options available for ages 3–18, CWR daily notes hope to help establish a firm foundation for children and young adults, enabling them to walk closely with God every day.

'My 11-year-old son has recently moved from the much-loved Topz *notes to* YP's*... I often learn a huge amount myself. His prayers are becoming more mature as we talk about what has come up.'*

To view CWR's whole range of youth and children's resources head to our website: **www.cwr.org.uk/resources**

Does God really care?

FOR READING & MEDITATION – JOB 5:6–7

'Yet man is born to trouble as surely as sparks fly upward.' (v7)

We move on now to try to answer the question: if God loves us so much, why is it that He allows so many seemingly bad things happen to us? I have found this to be the one question more than any other that troubles the hearts of so many. Time and time again I have sat before a weeping man or woman in whose life something tragic has happened and have heard them say: 'If God loves me, why did He let this happen?'

How can we keep our hearts open to God as the Ageless Romancer and trust His love when He seemingly allows so many hurtful things to happen? We have all lived through events that cause our hearts to ache – a faithless spouse, children who are unwell, parents who were not there for us, others chosen for jobs that we know we could do better, and so on. At such times, who has not cried out: 'God, why did You allow this to happen? Do you really care for me?' These are questions on which many a soul has been spiritually shipwrecked, leaving them grounded on reefs of pain and doubt.

Like me, you may have heard of or experienced personal tragedies within a family such as the loss of a loved one, perhaps through accident or illness. The emotional pain is intensified if that person is a child or a young person. The question we are often faced with at such times is: how could God allow such a thing to happen? No minister or counsellor finds it easy to answer. One man I know left the Christian ministry because he could not come up with an adequate answer to the question of why God allows bad things to happen to good people. If only we understood His heart more clearly.

FURTHER STUDY

Gen. 37:23–28;
39:1–20;
41:39–43;
45:3–11;
50:19–21

1. Who ensured that Joseph was sold as a slave in Egypt?

2. How did God's ultimate care bring initial pain?

My Father and my God, I know it is impossible for a human mind to comprehend all of Your ways, but help me to understand Your heart more deeply. I don't want to know answers so much, but I do want to know You. In Jesus' name I pray. Amen.

The wildness of God

FOR READING & MEDITATION – ISAIAH 2:1–11

'He will teach us his ways, so that we may walk in his paths.' (v3)

We continue exploring the question: if God loves us so much, why does He allow so many seemingly bad things to happen to us? 'What the Christian life all boils down to,' says a preacher friend, 'is this – can this love, which God says He has for us, be trusted?'

A counsellor tells how someone he was counselling spoke about how reckless and unpredictable God seemed to be in allowing tragic events to happen to her. She asked him: 'How can I trust a lover who is so wild?'

Walter Bruggeman, an American writer and theologian put it like this: 'We live our lives before the wild, dangerous, unfettered and free character of the living God.' Before reading that statement some years ago, I confess I had never thought of God in this way. The two authors I referred to earlier, Brent Curtis and John Eldridge, say in their book *The Sacred Romance*: 'There is something about God's rescues that make them a little less timely than dialling 911 [in the UK we dial 999]. He leaves Abraham with his knife raised and ready to plunge it into Isaac's heart and Isaac waiting for the knife to descend; he leaves Joseph languishing for years in an Egyptian prison; he allows the Israelites to suffer 400 years of bondage under the Egyptians and leaves those same Israelites backed against the Red Sea with Pharaoh's chariots thundering down on them. He abandons Jesus to the cross and does not rescue him at all.' You have to admit that God allows some pretty strange, even startling things to happen to His children. There can be no doubt about it – the Almighty's love for us really is wild.

FURTHER STUDY

Acts 16:6–40;
19:11–12;
2 Cor. 11:23–33

1. What was Paul's experience of God's ways?

2. Why did God allow Paul to be beaten and imprisoned?

Father, I see that I am to live my life before Your 'wild, dangerous unfettered and free character'. I feel a sense of awe and yet a little apprehension. I simply must understand more of this. Help me, my Father. In Jesus' name. Amen.

What's the theme?

FOR READING & MEDITATION – PSALM 107:1–16

'*Give thanks to the LORD, for he is good; his love endures for ever.*'
(v1)

The thought that God allows all kinds of unpleasant things to happen does not sit easily with some Christians, preferring to rationalise the issue rather than face it. They tell themselves such things as: 'the problems in my life must be there because of some sin I have committed' or 'I need to be more careful in the way I handle my life'.

To some extent and in some situations there might be some truth in these statements, but the issue is this: when we allow doubts about God's goodness to linger in our hearts, we live

FURTHER STUDY

Psa. 107:17–43;
Matt. 25:14–30;
Jonah 3:1–10

1. What theme ran through the unfaithful servant's heart?

2. What theme ran through his master's heart?

dangerously. We can, however, face our doubts and learn to answer the question, 'God, do you really care?' with certainty and confidence. I am convinced that the script by which many people live, especially those who have had more than their share of life's storms, is 'God is indifferent', rather than 'God is love'. Blaise Pascal said in his *Pensees*: 'The heart has its reasons that reason knows not of.' The head may say, 'I believe God is good', but if the heart is not convinced and says, 'God is indifferent', then the feelings in the heart hold sway.

One writer suggests that despite the many positive things Job said, there was a suspicion deep in his heart that God was indifferent. Job says, 'What I feared has come upon me; what I dreaded has happened to me' (Job 3:25). This writer says that Job was a God-fearing man, and yet he confesses to some insecurity. The words 'feared' and 'dreaded' are very strong. What theme runs through your heart – God is good, or God is indifferent? The psalmist in today's psalm has no doubt about it. How about you? Think carefully before you reply.

Father, help me look honestly into my heart. I want the theme of my heart to be in harmony with the theme of the psalmist that You are good. Let any doubt I may have about it be dissolved in the days ahead. In Jesus' name. Amen.

The light of day

FOR READING & MEDITATION – PSALM 139:1–24

'Search me, O God, and know my heart; test me and know my anxious thoughts.' (v23)

Every one of us has to come to grips with this issue of whether God is good and can be trusted; for how can we have an intimate relationship with God if we do not trust Him? Something that used to surprise me in the early days of my ministry as a pastor and counsellor was to discover how many experienced and seemingly mature Christians harboured, deep in their hearts, doubts about the goodness of God. But that was not the only surprise; the biggest one was to discover how they went about rationalising it.

I first came across this when a man, with over forty years' experience in the Christian life, came to me for counselling. He had gone through a series of great difficulties and problems, and was clearly wrestling with reconciling the goodness of God with the fact that so many bad things had recently happened to him. He said, 'God is not able to know everything that goes on all over the universe and some things slip into His children's lives unnoticed by Him.' This rationalisation worked for him, as it kept him from dealing with the question that was lodged deep in his heart after his bitter experiences: 'Does God really care for me?' He hid it in his heart, never allowing it to see the light of day. His rationalisation let him off the hook. It allowed him to believe that God was good, but not all-knowing.

FURTHER STUDY

1 Chron. 28:9;
Jer. 17:5–10;
23:23–24;
Luke 12:6–7,
22–34

1. What is the extent of God's knowledge?

2. Can anything in your life go unnoticed by God?

When we cover up our doubts beneath rationalisations, then quite simply we are not being honest. Integrity requires that whatever is true must be faced. We can't stop doubt rising in our hearts but if it is there we must face it and deal with it. Only recognised problems can be resolved.

Father, I would have no rationalisations, no subterfuges going on in my heart. If there are doubts about Your goodness, help me bring them to the surface and by Your grace face them and deal with them. In Jesus' name I pray. Amen.

No secret doubts

FOR READING & MEDITATION – PSALM 7:1–17

*'Judge me, O LORD, according to my righteousness,
according to my integrity, O Most High.' (v8)*

Yesterday we saw the futility of hiding our doubts about the goodness of God and attempting to deal with them through rationalisation. My dictionary defines rationalisation as 'bringing feelings into conformity with thinking'. Throughout the years, I have spent a lot of time exploring people's emotions in order to help them 'doubt their doubts and believe their beliefs'. Deep down in people's hearts, I have found grief-laden questions such as: God, why did you allow me to be born into a family that gave me no love? Why did You make me like this? Why did You allow so many bad things to happen to me? What will You allow to happen next?

FURTHER STUDY

Gen. 3:1–13;
1 Tim. 1:15–19

1. How did Satan sow the seeds of doubt in Adam and Eve?

2. What was the result?

If in the depths of our hearts we secretly believe that God did not protect us from bad things happening to us because He does not love us, then no matter how hard we try, we will fail to respond to His love and live life as God originally designed. Or, to put it another way, wrong beliefs about God will affect the way we feel about God, for how we think always influences the way we feel. So I say again: rationalisation is not a positive way of dealing with our doubts. We have to learn to face them, and bring them up and out. Living with secret doubts, fears or wrong beliefs in our hearts means we go through life with unnecessary apprehension and anxiety clinging to us. In turn, that will prevent us from entering into an intimate and passionate relationship with Jesus.

We are made in such a way that we cannot give ourselves to someone we do not trust. That is a simple, empirical fact. Don't let yourself be found in the category of those whose Christian lives have been sabotaged on the reefs of inner doubts and distrust.

Father, I see more clearly that if I am to live effectively and abundantly then every doubt about Your eternal goodness has to be dissolved. I bring all my doubts to You. Dissolve them in Your eternal love. In Jesus' name. Amen.

The stronger fire

FOR READING & MEDITATION – JEREMIAH 20:7–12

'O LORD, you deceived me, and I was deceived; you overpowered me and prevailed.' (v7)

What are we to make of God's wildness when bad things happen to us? 'Being in partnership with God', says Brent Curtis, 'often feels much more like being Mel Gibson's sidekick in *Lethal Weapon*. In his determination to meet with the bad guys, he leaps from seventh-storey balconies into swimming pools, surprised that we would have any hesitation in following after him.' Though God may be a 'wild lover', His purposes in allowing seemingly bad things to happen are consistent with His goodness. Unless we face that truth, we will live, as we said yesterday, with apprehension and anxiety tugging at our hearts. There can be nothing worse than living with the thought deep inside us: what will God allow to happen next? This fear can lay a cold hand on all our days.

FURTHER STUDY

Job 1:1–2:10;
Acts 2:1–4;
21:8–14

1. How did Job initially respond to adversity?

2. Why did Paul not fear death?

In the passage before us today, Jeremiah explodes with thoughts that have apparently been building up within him about God's use of him. Jeremiah, however, was a man of integrity. He was not only open to facing his doubts, but open also to facing the truth that God had built into his heart when He spoke to him as a young boy: 'Do not say, "I am only a child." You must go to everyone I send you to and say whatever I command you. Do not be afraid of them, for I am with you and will rescue you' (Jer. 1:7–8).

Jeremiah allowed his doubts to surface, but he also allowed the fire of that word that God had put into his heart to surface also. The fire that God had lit in his heart as a young boy was still burning despite the fire of doubt. Success in dealing with the fire of doubt that arises in the heart depends on which fire is the stronger.

Father, when doubts arise in my heart about Your goodness, grant that the fire of Your Word, which You have put there might rise up to extinguish all the flames of doubt, as it did in Jeremiah's heart. In Jesus' name. Amen.

'Is He safe?'

FOR READING & MEDITATION – ISAIAH 40:25–31

*'The LORD is the everlasting God... and his understanding
no-one can fathom.' (v28)*

We reflected the other day that Job was a good and godly man yet apparently he lived with an anxiety about what God might allow to happen to him. Something in him suspected that faith in God didn't necessarily mean peace and safety. It will help us, I think, to live more successfully if we come to terms with the fact that goodness is not necessarily synonymous with safety.

C.S. Lewis brings this out most powerfully in *The Lion, the Witch and the Wardrobe*. The four children in Lewis' story, Peter, Susan, Edmund and Lucy, pass through the wardrobe to find themselves in the kingdom of Narnia, which is under the spell of the white witch. Aslan, the king of Narnia is nowhere to be seen, although rumour has it he is 'on the move'. The children come upon Mr and Mrs Beaver, who are still faithful to Aslan. The Beavers assure the children that Aslan is about to return and put things right. The children wonder what Aslan is like. Lucy asks Mr Beaver if Aslan the Lion is safe. 'Safe? Who said anything about safe?' says Mr Beaver. 'Course he isn't safe. But he's good.'

FURTHER STUDY

Psa. 139:1–6;
Isa. 55:8–9;
Acts 27:1–28:31

1. Why did Paul feel safe in danger?

2. What is true safety?

Sometimes, the stakes in this world are very high, literally life or death. 'God', says one writer, 'rarely if ever cries "Cut" just as the dangerous or painful scene descends upon us.' We would like to picture goodness as synonymous with safety, but that is not the reality. And facing reality is the issue. When tragedy next strikes, we hold fast to the truth that there is some bigger purpose going on in the heart of our perfect God of love. Though it is beyond our ability to understand, it is nevertheless consistent with His goodness and love. Trust is not easy, but trust is the only answer.

Father, though You may not appear safe and I don't understand all Your purposes, I know that You are good. It's easy to say the words but no so easy to rest in them. I want to believe; help my unbelief. In Jesus' name. Amen.

The Achilles heel

FOR READING & MEDITATION – ROMANS 8:28–39

'And we know that in all things God works for the good of those who love him' (v28)

Why tragedies overtake God's children is without doubt one of the great mysteries of the universe. Accepting this mystery and not allowing it to sabotage our relationship with God is one of the biggest challenges of the Christian life.

In my early years as a Christian, whenever trouble or tragedy came my way, instead of accepting it as mystery, I tried to rationalise it. I told myself that this problem or difficulty might not have happened if I had been more careful, or if I had been more intent on ensuring that there was no sin in my life. Rationalisation dislikes mystery; it seeks to define it and explain it. When we do this we are really attempting to live comfortably rather than before the 'wild, dangerous, unfettered and free character of God'.

One of the most well-known rationalisations is that found in Rabbi Kushner's bestseller, *When Bad Things Happen to Good People*. Millions of people bought his book because it helped them come to terms with what Gore Vidal, an agnostic, described as the 'Achilles heel of Christianity – how can a God who is good allow bad things to happen in His world?' Rabbi Kushner answers the problem by saying that God is all good, but not all powerful. He claims that sin has so upset the mechanism of God's universe that He is powerless to stop bad things happening. His heart is inclined towards us, especially when He sees bad things coming our way, but because of sin, His universe has been disrupted and has now gone beyond His ability to intervene. I reject this argument, believing and understanding the Scriptures that teach that God is all good *and* all powerful. He could change things – but if He chooses not to, this never means He is not good.

FURTHER STUDY

Ruth 1; 4

1. How did God turn bad things to good in Ruth?

2. Compare Ruth and Orpah.

Father, help me recognise when so often I try to ease, by rationalisations, the discomfort in my heart that is there because of lack of trust. Forgive me and restore me to a life of trust. In Jesus' name. Amen.

How could God do that?

FOR READING & MEDITATION – JOB 1:1–22

'Have you considered my servant Job?... he is blameless and upright, a man who fears God and shuns evil.' (v8)

We continue asking ourselves: what are we to make of God's wildness in seeming to allow bad things to happen? Let's take a deeper look at the story of Job to see if we can understand a little more of the mystery.

The debate between God and Satan was over whether the foundation of God's kingdom was based on love or power. Astonishingly, God allows Satan to assail Job with all kinds of tragedies and places the perception of His own integrity on the response of Job's heart. This is how one commentator describes God's action in allowing Satan to unleash his evil ingenuity on the defenceless Job: 'This is very much akin to a policeman drawing the attention of a gang of thugs to a young man walking lawfully along the street with his wife, children and belongings. He then gives the gangsters permission to test the man's respect for the law by mugging and robbing him, and killing his children.' Graphic words, but they make a good point.

FURTHER STUDY

Psa. 74; 94

1. How did the psalmist express his confusion?

2. What were his conclusions?

I once conducted a group Bible study that centred on the story of Job. People in the group became greatly agitated as it unfolded. One made an excuse to leave the room. Others asked if we could turn to another subject. I sought to find out what was causing the agitation. Eventually it came out. One said: 'If God could do that to Job, what will stop Him doing the same thing with us? There is something frightening about a God who allows the devil to have his unhindered way in the life of one of His good-living children, causing them deep physical and emotional harm.' Faced with that question, I remember thinking I wished I had stayed in engineering. There, at least, one deals with problems for which there are clear answers.

My Father and my God, living before Your 'wild, dangerous, unfettered and free character' is indeed challenging. Breathe calm into my spirit, so that in the presence of the deepest mystery, I will be able to trust. In Jesus' name. Amen.

God is the answer

FOR READING & MEDITATION – JOB 42:1–17

'My ears had heard of you but now my eyes have seen you.' (v5)

How do we answer the problem raised in the group I talked about yesterday: why did God allow Job to be tested in such a hurtful way? There are really no final answers. Job is intent on getting some answers from God, but the Almighty comes to him with these words: 'Who is this that darkens my counsel with words without knowledge? Brace yourself like a man; I will question you, and you shall answer me' (Job 38:2–3).

This is followed by a lengthy questioning of Job's understanding of creation. 'Where were you when I laid the earth's foundation? Tell me, if you understand. Who marked off its dimensions? Surely you know!' (vv4–5). How cold and unfeeling these words appear at first. God is seemingly saying: 'Don't question me; I know what I am doing. And what I do is good. Trust me.'

Have you noticed that God never repents for anything He does? This is essentially because everything He does is right. Job however is repentant; he is contrite over his wrong thoughts about God (42:3). Then he goes away with a sense of: 'Ah, now I get it… the God who made the universe is powerful enough to have saved me from all my catastrophes and the reason He did not do so is known only to Him. I trust Him enough to know that whatever He does is good and right.' Though God did not give Job any answers, He gave him a revelation of Himself. For Job this was enough. It was as if God said, 'I will not give you answers, but I will give you me.' God then spoke with Job's friends. He tells them quite plainly that they know nothing about Him (v7). Then He tells them that He will have Job pray for them. Job does and releases his own life and those of others (v10).

FURTHER STUDY

Rom. 9:1–33;
11:22–36;
2 Cor. 12:7–10;
2 Tim. 2:13;
Heb. 13:5–6

1. How logical is God?

2. How faithful is God?

Father, thank You that in the presence of mystery You do not give answers but You give Yourself. That is better than any answer. I would rather have You and no answers than have answers but not You. Amen.

No better context

FOR READING & MEDITATION – JOHN 9:1–12

'Neither this man nor his parents sinned... but this happened so that the work of God might be displayed' (v3)

Today's text is one to come to terms with if we are to overcome the barriers that prevent us from believing deep in our hearts that God is good. It is not too difficult to believe that the wounds and hurts we receive in life are the result of our own choices and thoughtlessness. But when we are told that certain things that we would label as 'tragedies' are brought about directly by the hand of God, we feel perplexed or confused.

When Jesus and His disciples were walking on the road, they met a man who was born blind. 'His disciples asked him,

FURTHER STUDY

John 11:1–53;
Rom. 8:18–25

1. Why did Lazarus have to die?

2. How did people react to the miracle?

"Rabbi, who sinned, this man or his parents, that he was born blind?" "Neither this man nor his parents sinned," said Jesus, "but this happened so that the work of God might be displayed in his life"' ('made manifest', KJV). Having said this, Jesus spat on the ground, made some mud to put on the man's eyes, and sent him to wash in the Pool of Siloam. When he did so he was healed.

What did He mean – that the works of God might be made manifest? Ah, here we are in the presence of mystery. The answer to that is still to be revealed. Theologians struggle to explain how God's character is revealed through the seemingly bad things that He allows to go on in His world, but no one has found adequate answers. Faced with mystery, we need healing – not to see but to believe. How God works through the wounds, the losses, the suffering and the tragedies that come into our lives is something we will never fully know on this earth. We are big enough to ask the questions, but not big enough to understand the answers. And so we groan and we wonder, but in our groaning and wonderment there is really no better context for trust.

Father, help me to grasp this – the muscles of faith are not exercised if not challenged. It is in the presence of mystery that I find the best context for trust. Drive this truth deep into my spirit, dear Lord. In Jesus' name. Amen.

The team in Cambodia

CWR Asia

In recent years, CWR's counselling courses in South East Asia have extended from Singapore to Cambodia. We feel privileged to serve the Church (and pastoral workers) in a country where psychotherapy is a new concept, and the wounds of hurt and suffering from the recent history of the Khmer Rouge run deep. The need for pastoral training and support is huge, and through the generous support of donations, CWR has seen many students through four core modules of counselling training delivered in English – and this year, for the first time, the teaching will be delivered in Khmer, extending the reach to even more people.

'The skills and information I have gained from this course have proven invaluable – both in my own life and in walking alongside others.' Missionary, Cambodia

'This pastoral counselling course is really healing some brokenness in my life, and it helps with self-awareness. I would love to reach out to the broken-hearted people in Cambodia. Thank you so much for providing this course to the Cambodian people.'
Counselling student, Cambodia

Thank you for your continuing prayers and support for this vital work in South East Asia.
www.cwr.org/asia

A vital question

FOR READING & MEDITATION – 1 CHRONICLES 29:10–20

'I know, my God, that you test the heart and are pleased with integrity.' (v17)

We turn now to ask the question: what if we don't (or won't) accept the truth that whatever happens to us is part of God's good and loving purposes? The answer is that our hearts are open to being seduced by other lovers.

My experience as a minister and a counsellor for many years convinces me that many Christians struggle with repressed feelings of disappointment. Things have happened in their lives that, deep down, they believe God should have protected them from. These repressed feelings then prevent them from entering into a passionate relationship with God. It is difficult, as I have said, to be intimately involved with someone whom you do not believe has your best interests at heart.

The last few days have been challenging and searching, I know, but now let us face the issue more fully and ask ourselves a personal question. Are there repressed and forgotten disappointments reverberating within me because of seemingly bad things God has allowed to happen in my life? Find a quiet place and go over your life, asking yourself: Am I free of all disappointments against God for seemingly bad things that happened to me? Invite His Holy Spirit to help you. If you are conscious of disappointment, it is likely that beneath it might be a lingering resentment. That resentment acts like an infection in your subconscious, poisoning your attitudes. If resentment is there, confess it to Him. Ask Him to puncture and press out the poison and bring your soul to perfect health. Today could be the day that makes all other days different.

FURTHER STUDY

Jer. 4:14–22;
Heb. 12:14–29;
James 3:8–18;
Hab. 3:16–19

1. What power can disappointment and bitterness exercise over us?

2. Invite the Holy Spirit to free you of any resentment.

My Father and my God, I have lived on denials and defences for far too long. Now I want to be free – free to live before Your wild and dangerous character with trust in Your love and goodness. Help me, dear Father. In Jesus' name. Amen.

Redemptive busyness

FOR READING & MEDITATION – JAMES 1:19–27

*'Do not merely listen to the word, and so deceive yourselves.
Do what it says.' (v22)*

Yesterday we considered that when we refuse to accept that whatever God allows to happen in our lives is part of His perfect purposes, then our hearts are open to being seduced by other lovers. Time and again I have dealt with people who say they don't feel much love in their hearts for Jesus any more. I have often found the cause to be repressed disappointments toward God for allowing something in their lives that they believe He should have protected them from. Repressed disappointments are a major reason for increasing distance from God, and can lead to a root of bitterness.

It is characterised by: not much spiritual feeling in prayer; no desire to weep with those who weep or rejoice with those who rejoice; no engagement when among worshippers (either with them, or with God); inappropriate fantasies; occasional feelings of depression; outbursts of anger; irritation, and an ever-present anxiety. Clearly, these responses could arise from other root causes, such as a malfunctioning physiology, or as the result of divine conviction that comes from engaging in continued sinful practices. These things apart, however, the signs I have described will often be present in the life of someone whose heart is tormented with forgotten and undealt with disappointments giving rise to resentment.

FURTHER STUDY

Luke 10:38–42;
15:25–30

1. How did Martha show 'redemptive busyness'?

2. Describe the attitudes of Martha and the elder brother.

The remedy isn't to redouble your efforts at Christian disciplines, such as prayer, extra Bible reading, or by taking up Christian activities like children's or youth work and so on – what someone has described as 'redemptive busyness'. The cause must be traced, confessed, rooted out and brought up. Nothing else will do.

Lord, I see that my life will be made or broken at the place where I meet and deal with repressed disappointments. Help me not to run from them, but to tackle them. In Jesus' name I pray. Amen.

The dynamics of seduction

FOR READING & MEDITATION – EPHESIANS 4:17–30

'*Do not let the sun go down while you are still angry, and do not give the devil a foothold.*' (vv26–27)

Today we consider what exactly are these 'other lovers' waiting to seduce our hearts when we don't allow Jesus to be the true lover of our souls. Before exploring them, let's unpack the dynamics that make the soul vulnerable to seduction. Our souls have been designed for a divine romance. When we fail to engage with Christ, the Ageless Romancer, pain arises within our personalities – the pain of non-engagement, of non-being. This pain, like all pain, cries out to be appeased. If Jesus is not allowed to fill our souls with His love and presence then we will look to other sources to ease the pain.

FURTHER STUDY

2 Cor. 2:1–11;
11:14;
Eph. 6:10–18;
James 4:7;
1 Pet. 5:8–9

1. How do we ensure that Satan does not seduce us?

2. What are his strategies?

One way in which Satan attempts to seduce us is to encourage us to indulge in emotions that give us false comfort. Such emotions are lust, anger, self-pity, false guilt, and so on. These emotions protect us from feelings of grief, loneliness, abandonment, disappointment, desperate longing and true guilt. The emotions I have just described are powerful motivators to the soul. They motivate us, if we let them, towards recognising that our lives are empty without God and that He is our only hope. Satan seduces us to replace emotions that will turn us God-wards with feelings that are self-indulgent.

Why do we fall for it? Because anger, for example, is a more delicious feeling than disappointment, and self-pity is a better painkiller for the soul's pain than loneliness. There is much more hope for us when we allow ourselves to feel the uncomfortable emotions which lead us to throw ourselves at the feet of God.

Father, help me to stand against the temptation of the devil. I surrender my emotions to You – help me to be on my guard, and not to allow the enemy in. You have my will, give me Your strength. In Jesus' name. Amen.

False comforters

FOR READING & MEDITATION – PSALM 119:73–80

'May your unfailing love be my comfort, according to your promise to your servant.' (v76)

We look now at another lover that Satan uses to seduce our souls – addiction. In his book *Addiction and Grace*, Gerald May says: 'Addiction is the most powerful psychic enemy of humanity's desire for God and is one of our adversary's favourite ways of imprisoning us.'

What is addiction, and how does it happen? Let me see if I can explain how it operates in the life of the soul. The nerve endings of our souls cry out to be satisfied. This is how God has designed us. We are made to taste transcendence. If God is not at work in our souls, pouring His life-giving water into us, then we look for some form of immediate satisfaction, something that will bring a cool taste to our parched spiritual tongues. It can come from anything: an affair, drugs, obsessions, pornography, promiscuity, or even living off our professional expertise or giftedness. These things have the same effect on our souls as crack cocaine on the body. Once we allow our hearts to taste these things, to bring false comfort to our souls, they can soon overpower our will.

FURTHER STUDY

John 8:31–36;
Rom. 6:1–8:4

1. What are the dynamics of spiritual slavery?

2. How can we be free?

The French writer Jean-Jacques Rousseau said that nothing is less in power than the heart; far from commanding it, we are forced to obey it. If we allow ourselves to be taken captive by an addiction, whether it be to sport or sex, trying to free ourselves by willpower alone is ineffective. Only admission of our enslavement and a repentant heart will release God to aid us. We cry out to God and call upon His name. It is the Holy Spirit alone who can save us. He is the only one who can bring us to our senses. Our heart will either carry us to God or it will carry us to addiction.

My Father God, You are my centre and my circumference. In You I am kept steady and growing. Help me to find the comfort I need in You, dear Father. Then I shall not need false comforters. In Jesus' name. Amen.

Stay at home

FOR READING & MEDITATION – JOHN 15:1–17

'If you remain in me and my words remain in you, ask whatever you wish, and it will be given you.' (v7)

I hope it is becoming clearer day by day that when we do not rest in the love that Jesus has for us, then we become vulnerable to other lovers. Once, in my reading, I came across the testimony of a man who found his 'lover' to be cynicism and rebellion.

He says: 'I began to notice that when I was tired or anxious, there were certain sentences I would say in my head that led me to a very familiar place. The journey would often start with me walking around disturbed, feeling as if there was something deep inside that I needed to put into words but couldn't. I would start to say things like "Life stinks… Why is it always so hard?… It's never going to change… Who cares?… Life is a joke…" Surprisingly, I noticed by the time I was saying those last sentences that I was feeling better, the anxiety would greatly diminish.' The cynicism and rebellion acted for him, you see, like some sort of soul drug. Later he came to see that it was an alternative spiritual abiding place; this 'lover' was another comforter, another love.

FURTHER STUDY

John 14:15–23;
1 John 2:1–6,
24–29; 3:4–7

1. How do we abide in Christ?

2. What is the result?

The light came on when he read the words of the text before us today in *The Message*, which renders it: 'If you make yourselves at home with me and my words are at home in you, you can be sure that whatever you ask will be listened to and acted upon.' Jesus seemed to be saying to him through these words: 'I have made my home in you, but you have not made your home in me. You have other comforters to which you go. You need to learn to make your home in me.' Staying at 'home', he found resting in the love of Jesus to be the secret of overcoming cynicism and rebellion.

Lord Jesus, save me from these false comforters that promise so much but give so little. I see that the secret is to abide in You, to 'stay at home', so to speak. May my abiding place always be in You. In Your name I pray. Amen.

'There ain't no living left'

FOR READING & MEDITATION – JOHN 7:34–44

'Jesus stood and said in a loud voice, "If a man is thirsty, let him come to me and drink".' (v37)

Harold Horton ministered in the Assemblies of God movement during the first half of the twentieth century. In his book *Chords from Solomon's Song* (now out of print), Horton wrote: 'If only we could learn to rest in the love of our Lord we would have no need to recourse to the overtures of other lovers.'

The true spiritual life is more than keeping away from bad habits and actions, or even doing good works. As we have been seeing, it means learning to abide in Christ. If we do not abide in Him then we will abide in something else. The man I referred to yesterday whose abiding place was cynicism and rebellion went on to say: 'From my abiding place I would feel free to use some soul cocaine: a violence video with maybe a little sexual titillation thrown in, perhaps having a little more alcohol with a meal than I might normally drink – things that would allow me to feel better for just a little while. I had always thought of these things as just bad habits. I began to see they were much more.'

When our souls are not in tune or in touch with the love that flows towards us from Jesus Christ, we have two options. One is to try to satisfy the pain that arises from the absence of God's love by indulging our appetites. The other is to anaesthetise it. Permit me to ask you this question: if you do not abide in Jesus, then where do you abide? 'There is only one being who can satisfy the last aching abyss of the human heart,' said Oswald Chambers, 'and that is our Lord Jesus Christ.' Jimi Hendrix, the 1960s guitarist idolised by the masses, said before dying of a drug overdose: 'There ain't no living left nowhere.' Outside of Jesus Christ, there ain't!

FURTHER STUDY

Jer. 2:9–37;
John 5:36–40;
6:47–69

1. What methods do we use to comfort our souls?

2. How do we drink of Jesus?

God, if I have been relying on false comforters to alleviate the pain in my soul that comes from lack of contact with You, forgive me, I pray. I want to be wholly and entirely reliant on You. In Jesus' name I ask it. Amen.

Who is in control?

FOR READING & MEDITATION – GENESIS 3:1–19

'Because you listened to your wife and ate from the tree...
Cursed is the ground because of you' (v17)

Yesterday we saw that when our souls are not in tune or in touch with the love that flows towards us from Jesus Christ, we to try to find other ways to satisfy the pain that arises, or we try to anaesthetise it. Let's explore now another way of anaesthetising pain in the soul: by competency and control. I know people who feel that life has no meaning for them unless everything that goes on in their lives is under their control. It expresses itself in such ways as a clean desk, a spotless house, a perfectly manicured lawn, a tidy garage, a dinner party where nothing goes wrong. They have a two- or three-step formula for answering every spiritual problem, and so on.

FURTHER STUDY

Eccl. 1:12–4:8;
12:13

1. By what methods did Solomon try to find life?

2. What were the results and his conclusions?

There is nothing wrong in being competent or in control of things *per se*. The danger arises when we make that our route to life. I am always intrigued by today's passage, where God is explaining to the first human pair that never again will they be in perfect control. Adam would find resistance from thorns and thistles in his attempt to master and dominate the earth. Eve would find childbirth painful and she would desire to control her husband but her efforts would fail (v16).

I believe that, in part, the purpose was to discourage them from thinking that their lives could ever work without returning to the original design of full and utter dependence on God; of abiding in Him, living by His resources rather than their own. God's intentions here may seem harsh and even cruel, but we must remember that Satan's offer to Eve was that she could bring about her own redemption through knowing good and evil. Life is not found in control; life is found in God.

Father, day after day I see You want my heart to rest in You and only in You. How far from the truth I have been to believe that there are other routes to life than You. Forgive me and instruct me further. In Jesus' name. Amen.

Free!

FOR READING & MEDITATION – GALATIANS 5:1–15

*'It is for freedom that Christ has set us free. Stand firm, then,
and do not let yourselves be burdened again' (v1)*

We spend another day on this issue of control. Yesterday's meditation needs a little clarification. Perhaps the best way we can do this is to X-ray, so to speak, a soul that is bent on control as a way of living. We can then see something of its inner dynamics. It would show, I think, a soul preoccupied with what we described as 'redemptive busyness', so that all pain is kept at bay. If it were possible to interpret the motivations of a soul held together by control, we would probably hear such things as: 'My soul hurts for want of romance. But as I am not in touch with my Ageless Romancer in the way my soul aches for, I will settle for less. I will avoid the wildness of God by something less wild. I will keep my life under strict control. It may not give me the satisfaction I long for but at least it will dull the painful ache in my soul for a close relationship with God.'

FURTHER STUDY

Gal. 2:20–4:31

1. What are the benefits of rules and routine?

2. What are the dangers?

I used to live by control, but I am glad that Jesus lifted me out of it. After a first session of counselling, a woman who had a serious marital problem said: 'You have been more help to me in this one session than all the other people I have consulted.' After she left I felt deeply anxious and so I considered what was going on in my heart. My false lover was saying to me, 'You had better keep coming up with fresh new insights or you will not be valued.' The text at the top of the page came home to me with new force. I said to myself: 'Selwyn Hughes, for you to live is not Christ but control. You are depending on your counselling insights to hold your soul together, not your relationship with your Lord.' The next step was repentance. From that day, I have been free.

Lord God, You have not fashioned us in our inmost being and then abandoned us to pressures too strong for us. You continually give us wake-up calls that remind us of our need to stay close to You. Thank You, dear Father. Amen.

Fearing the unknown

FOR READING & MEDITATION – EPHESIANS 1:3–23

'I keep asking that... God... may give you the Spirit of wisdom and revelation, so that you may know him better.' (v17)

It's all too easy to allow our hearts to be seduced by other lovers. Forgive the repetition, but this point needs to be stressed again and again. If we think that life is found elsewhere than in God then we become easy prey for other comforters.

God wants us to come back to the same relational intimacy that existed between Him and Adam and Eve in the Garden of Eden, before they were deceived by Satan. Part of us longs to experience deep relational intimacy with God; after all, that is what our souls are designed for. But while we long for it, we fear the unknowns of walking in close communion with God. So we settle for things that bring some degree of satisfaction or lessen the pain in our souls. It is possible to focus on spiritual exercises like Bible study, giving away Christian resources, and other forms of Christian service, as a way of bringing satisfaction to our soul. These things can become other lovers.

FURTHER STUDY

2 Cor. 3:12–18;
Eph. 3:1–21;
Col. 1:15–27

1. What is the mystery of Christ?

2. How do we come to love Christ's love more deeply?

Am I saying that being occupied with the things of God are unimportant? Of course not. But they can become our point of dependency. Whenever we become even partly convinced that our life is elsewhere other than in a direct intimate relationship with God, we are self-deceived. C.S. Lewis says in *Weight of Glory*: 'We are half-hearted creatures fooling about with drink and sex and ambition [he could also have said religious effort] when infinite joy is offered us, like an ignorant child who wants to go on making mud pies in a slum because he cannot imagine what is meant by the offer of a holiday at the sea. We are far too easily pleased.' Nothing will ever satisfy our soul other than God. *Nothing!*

Father, save me from settling for less than the knowledge of You. Help me understand that though spiritual exercises are important I must not put them ahead of my relationship with You. You alone are to be my dependency. Amen.

Listen to your heart

FOR READING & MEDITATION – MATTHEW 11:25–30

*'Come to me, all you who are weary and burdened,
and I will give you rest.' (v28)*

It is simply heartbreaking to see Christians who, as C.S. Lewis put it in yesterday's quote, are 'too easily pleased'. God has put within our hearts a desire and longing for Him that is wild; it will never be satisfied with other lovers. It is easier sometimes to go through religious routines and duties – and these have their place – but when these become a safe substitute for being taken up into the arms of our Lover in a deeply personal way, it is a poor exchange. 'If we could listen to our heart', says one spiritual director, 'it would tell us how weary it is of the familiar and the indulgent.'

Jesus invites us into close communion with Him, to heart-to-heart engagement, but we hear His words and yet pull back. Why? Often we are afraid that He might do the same to our hearts as others might have done: loved us and then left us. Who has not been disappointed in love? These experiences set us up for self-protection. We say to ourselves, 'I will never give anyone the power to hurt me again. I may give them part of my heart, but I will not give them all of it.' How sad it is when we adopt that same attitude towards God. He alone can love us in the way our heart craves. In *Batter my Heart*, John Donne has a prayer that all of us would do well to pray if we have been seduced by other lovers:

> *Yet dearly I love you, and would be loved fain*
> *But I am betrothed unto your enemy*
> *Divorce me, untie, or break that knot again*
> *Take me to you, imprison me, for I,*
> *Except you enthral me, shall never be free,*
> *Nor ever chaste except you ravish me.*

FURTHER STUDY

Psa. 95;
Isa. 55:1–7;
Hosea 6:1–3;
Matt. 15:1–14

1. What is involved when we come to God?

2. How did the Pharisees love religion but not God?

My Father and my God, shatter any chain that binds me to a false lover. No longer will I be betrothed to Your enemy. I would be Yours and Yours alone. This I ask in and through Your Son's powerful and peerless name. Amen.

Hearing with Israel's ears

FOR READING & MEDITATION – JEREMIAH 2:1–25

'How can you say, "I am not defiled; I have not run after the Baals"?…
consider what you have done.' (v23)

Verse 13 of today's passage clearly identifies God's astonishment with His people: they have forsaken Him and 'dug their own cisterns'. In the context of our thoughts over the past few days, they have been seduced by other lovers. Let's ask ourselves: how does He feel when the fire of our love for Him cools and becomes nothing more than grey ash; when we have allowed ourselves to be seduced by other lovers?

The graphic picture before us today reveals exactly how He feels. This is how the Living Bible paraphrases it: 'O restless female camel, seeking for a male! You are a wild donkey, sniffing the wind at mating time… Any [male] wanting you need not search, for you come running to him! Why don't you turn from all this weary running after other gods? But you say, "Don't waste your breath, I've fallen in love with these strangers and I can't stop loving them now!"' (vv24–25). God is saying in effect: 'I love you, but you are pulling away from me. Another lover seems to have captured your heart.' Israel's answer, like that of any one addicted to another love is: 'It's no use, I love foreign gods and I must go after them.'

FURTHER STUDY

Isa. 1:1–2:8;
Jer. 3:1–4:31

1. Why does God ask us to argue with Him?

2. Why did Israel often pursue other lovers?

Am I speaking to someone today who has taken another lover into their heart? God aches over you as He did over Israel. He holds out His hand to you today and says: 'Come back, give up your other lovers, come and live with me and let us be lovers once again.' Over and over again in the Old Testament, God tries to engage Israel in a lover's quarrel. Israel, of course, kept hearing His words as an attack on how they were going about their duties. Those with seduced hearts 'hear God with Israel's ears'.

Father, You want for Yourself the inmost shrine – me. So I reject from my heart today all other lovers. I am Yours. Amen.

Our True Identity

There are many things in life that might shape our identity, or bring confusion to our sense of self. But what does the Bible say about who we really are? What kind of people does God intend us to become?

As children of God, our true identity is one based on who we are in Christ – and not by what our culture, career or circumstances tell us. In this issue, discover how to know yourself and God better, and how to let the characteristics of your new identity show.

Every Day **with Jesus**

MAY/JUN 2018

Our True Identity

'Therefore, if anyone is in Christ, he is a new creation; the old has gone, the new has come!'
2 Corinthians 5:17

Living life with Jesus. Every day   CWR

Also available as eBook/ eSubscription

Obtain your copy from CWR, a Christian bookshop or your National Distributor.
If you would like to take out a subscription, see the order form at the back of these notes.

Adrenaline for the soul!

FOR READING & MEDITATION – HEBREWS 12:1–13

'Let us fix our eyes on Jesus, the author and perfecter of our faith'
(v2)

How did Jesus maintain a passionate heart in the midst of all the opposition that faced Him? If we uncover this truth, then we too might be able to live with passion, no matter what obstacles might confront us. The last week of His life on earth reveals the passion that pulsed through His soul. He clears the temple of the merchants who had turned His Father's house into 'a den of robbers' (Matt. 21:13). Later, He stands looking over the city that He loved so much and cries: 'O Jerusalem... how often have I longed to gather your children together, as a hen gathers her chicks under her wings, but you were not willing' (Matt. 23:37). Later still, He meets with His disciples for a special meal, and He says, 'I have eagerly desired to eat this Passover with you before I suffer' (Luke 22:15). There is passion and intensity too in the Gethsemane prayer, and of course, the cross.

FURTHER STUDY

Heb. 2:1– 4:16

1. List some of the qualities of Jesus.

2. Why did the Son of God experience human struggles?

How did Jesus sustain His passion? One answer I think is found in the text before us today. *The Message* puts it like this: 'Keep your eyes on Jesus, who both began and finished this race we're in. Study how he did it. Because he never lost sight of where he was headed – that exhilarating finish in and with God – he could put up with anything along the way: cross, shame, whatever. And now he's *there*, in the place of honor, right alongside God. When you find yourselves flagging in your faith, go over that story again, item by item, that long litany of hostility he plowed through. *That* will shoot adrenaline into your souls!'

Jesus kept in mind where He was heading and wanted to get there with all His heart. These two themes were what kept Him moving onward. They will keep us moving too.

Lord Jesus Christ, what an inspiration You are in my life. Help me to keep You as my central focus, to glance at other things but to gaze only upon You. For Your own dear name's sake. Amen.

A birthday hymn

FOR READING & MEDITATION – JOHN 13:1–17

'I have set you an example that you should do as I have done for you.'
(v15)

We saw yesterday that two themes dominated the life of Jesus, enabling Him to move through all the difficulties and problems that confronted Him. He remembered where He was heading, and He wanted to get there with all His heart. I know of nowhere in the Gospels where this truth is highlighted more than in the passage before us now. John tells us that Jesus, knowing 'that he had come from God and was returning to God… wrapped a towel round his waist… poured water into a basin and began to wash his disciples' feet' (vv3–5). He knew where He had come from and where He was going. This enabled Him to live His life of passion and selfless love right to the end.

It is said that Charles Wesley wrote in total some seven thousand hymns, and of these a goodly number were composed to mark the major happenings in his own life. Among such occasional pieces is one of his best known and best loved hymns, which he wrote on one of his birthdays. It begins:

Away with our fears, the glad morning appears
When an heir of salvation is born
From Jehovah I came, for His glory I am,
And to Him I with singing return.

From Jehovah I came? Where does his father Samuel Wesley come in? And of course his heroic mother Susannah? Had he forgotten them? Oh, no! He was not being unmindful of them. But, as he glances back over the years, he sees that he came not merely from the love that had joined together his father and mother but from the love that had set the great redemptive plan in motion: the love of God.

FURTHER STUDY

John 1:1–13; 3:3–8; 8:14; 14:1–3; 1 John 5:1–12

1. Where have we come from?

2. Where are we going?

Father, how can I thank You enough that I am caught up in a story that began in the eternity past and will end in the eternity to come. 'From Jehovah I came, for His glory I am.' How wonderful. Thank You, Father. Amen.

Singing the genealogy

FOR READING & MEDITATION – 1 JOHN 3:1–10

*'But we know that when he appears, we shall be like him,
for we shall see him as he is.' (v2)*

We continue reflecting on the thought that, if we are to live with passion, then we need to remember where we have come from, and we need to know where we are going. Yesterday we saw how Charles Wesley celebrated one of his birthdays by singing his genealogy as a son of God. He saw far beyond his earthly parentage. 'From Jehovah I came', he wrote, 'and to Him I with singing return.' The Bible writers often do the same. No sooner do they touch this thrilling theme of our spiritual genealogy than their language trembles on the verge of song. John, for example, in our reading today cries jubilantly, 'Dear friends, now we are children of God'. The King James Version puts it like this: 'Beloved, now are we the sons of God'.

FURTHER STUDY

Rom. 8:14–17;
Gal. 3:26–4:7;
1 Pet. 1:17–23

1. How do we become sons of God?

2. What are the privileges and responsibilities?

Listen to the apostle Paul on the same theme: 'For you did not receive a spirit that makes you a slave again to fear, but you received the Spirit of sonship. And by him we cry, "*Abba*, Father"' (Rom. 8:15). The classic text on this subject is found in Paul's letter to the Ephesians: 'For he chose us in him before the creation of the world... In love he predestined us to be adopted as his sons through Jesus Christ, in accordance with his pleasure and will – to the praise of his glorious grace, which he has freely given us in the One he loves' (Eph. 1:4–6).

It was said of the Puritans that they so valued and revered the Word of God that they set even the genealogies to music. Singing a genealogy – think of that! Could we do it? I rather doubt it. Be that as it may, there is one genealogy which is certainly something to sing about – our genealogy as children of God.

Father, I want to tell You from my heart that nothing means more to me than being Your child. I am sorry that I do not make more of it in my heart. Help me live in the consciousness of this glorious and important fact. In Jesus' name. Amen.

God's pleasure

FOR READING & MEDITATION – 1 CORINTHIANS 9:19–27

*'Do you not know that in a race... only one gets the prize?
Run in such a way as to get the prize.' (v24)*

We are saying that two themes are to grip us if we are to journey through this world with spiritual passion – remembering where we came from and where we are going. The writer and psychologist Dan Allender asks: 'How can we reclaim the treasures of memory for our life's journey?'

The text we looked at the other day from Hebrews 12:2–3 gives us the clue. Let us look at it again as it is in *The Message*: 'Keep your eyes on *Jesus*, who both began and finished this race we're in. Study how he did it. Because he never lost sight of where he was headed – that exhilarating finish in and with God – he could put up with anything along the way: cross, shame, whatever. And now he's *there*, in the place of honor, right alongside God. When you find yourself flagging in your faith, go over that story again, item by item, that long litany of hostility he plowed through. *That* will shoot adrenaline into your souls!'

Do you need some adrenaline pumped into your soul? Then study how Jesus ran the race that was set before Him. As we have already seen, He knew where He came from and He knew where He was going. Jesus ran because of 'the joy set before him' (Heb. 12:2). Without these two themes dominating our lives – remembering where we came from and where we are going – we will not run well, perhaps not even walk! The film *Chariots of Fire* is about two Olympic runners, Eric Liddell and Harold Abrahams. Both are passionate about running, but Abrahams runs because he is driven; Liddell runs because, as he says, 'When I run I feel God's pleasure.' How do you run? Because you have to, or because you feel God's pleasure?

FURTHER STUDY

Gal. 5:7;
Phil. 2:5–16;
3:7–14;
2 Tim. 4:7–8

1. How do sports metaphors help us understand Christianity?

2. What obstacles do you have to overcome in your own race?

Jesus, source of all joy, help me run the race that is before me with the same victorious vitality that characterised Your life when You were here on earth. For Your own dear name's sake. Amen.

The best piece of advice

FOR READING & MEDITATION – PSALM 25

'My eyes are ever on the LORD, for only he will release my feet from the snare.' (v15)

Nothing enables us to run the race that is set before us more effectively than focusing on the life of our Master. 'Study how He did it', said the writer to the Hebrews. Rehearse the story; go over it item by item. Dr Martyn Lloyd-Jones said: 'The worst affliction that can beset the human heart is forgetfulness. We would forget the death of our Lord were it not that we are called back to it constantly through the table of communion.' Perhaps…

Let's put it another way: the worst affliction that can beset the human heart is the failure to remember. In a week's time most of what you have read in this present issue will be forgotten, but what must not be forgotten, what you must keep ever before you, is the way Jesus lived His life.

FURTHER STUDY

Matt. 4:1–11;
16:21–23;
Mark 14:32–42;
Luke 22:39–46

1. How did Jesus deal with temptation?

2. How did Jesus deal with difficult choices?

We are touching here one of the great lessons of effective Christian living. I am afraid new followers of Jesus never seem to get introduced to it. In the early days of my Christian walk, my pastor drummed it into me. 'Keep remembering the way Jesus lived His life,' he would say. 'Never forget how He kept referring to His past and His future. It kept Him steady and it will keep you steady too.' When I am asked, 'What was the greatest piece of advice you were ever given?' I give that as my answer. Jesus never lost sight of where He came from and where He was heading – and neither must we.

We were conceived in the heart of the Trinity to be His lovers, and we are heading towards the consummation of all our hopes and desires – a meeting with our Lover. No matter what happens, keep that clear thought ever before you. That is the best piece of advice I can give you.

God, watch over my spirit and keep it from growing tired. Help me live with the thought ever before me that Your plans for me were conceived in eternity past and will be consummated in eternity to come. Amen.

The vision of heaven

SUN
29 APR

FOR READING & MEDITATION – PHILIPPIANS 1:12–30

'For to me, to live is Christ and to die is gain.' (v21)

St Augustine said, 'The whole life of the good Christian is a holy longing.' A longing for what? It is a longing, as we said yesterday, for the culmination of all our hopes and desires when we see Jesus and are joined to Him forever. Some Christians maintain that we ought to think more about earth than we do of heaven. 'Live to make the earth a better place,' they say, 'and heaven will take care of itself.' There is some truth in that of course, but study the lives of the saints of the past, and you will find that they kept alive in their hearts the desire for heaven.

Jesus has gone on before us. He is there right now. What kept Him moving towards the goal, 'enduring the cross, scorning its shame'? The joy that was set before Him. We do not neglect our duties and responsibilities here on earth but I don't believe we will ever run the race effectively unless we keep the vision of heaven always before us. The deeper the desire for heaven grows within us, the more adrenaline, to use Eugene Peterson's words, will be shot into our souls.

FURTHER STUDY

Rev. 4:1–5:14; 21:1–7; 22:1–6

1. What do you find most exciting about heaven?

2. Why is a vision of heaven important?

One Christian testifies as to how the prospect of heaven influences his daily living: 'I am a fortunate man. My friends and family love me, but sometimes they let me down. When I feel the pain of their failure I can retreat into cynicism (isn't this the way life is?), or become more demanding (you must never do that to me again). Or, I can let it be a reminder that a day is coming when we will all live in perfect love. I can let the ache lead me deeper into my heart and higher toward heaven'. This is how Jesus lived, and so can we.

Father, help me keep the vision of heaven before me. Tune my heart so that it is like the apostle Paul's – eager to go but willing to stay. Perhaps I am more eager to stay than willing to go. Help me examine my heart. In Jesus' name. Amen.

We'll soon be home

FOR READING & MEDITATION – SONG OF SONGS 2:14–17
'My lover is mine and I am his' (v16)

O n our last day together exploring the theme of 'a higher love', we remind ourselves of what we have discovered. God is a Lover at heart, and underlying the universe there is a passionate purpose. The Christian life is not just carrying out certain duties and responsibilities – it is being invited into an intimate relationship. Duties and responsibilities are important of course, but as G.K. Chesterton says: 'Romance is the deepest thing in life, romance is deeper even than reality.' It is. We are the objects of a passionate lover; we are the pursued.

FURTHER STUDY

1 Cor. 13;
1 Thess.
4:13–18;
Heb. 6:11–20

1. How did Stephen react as he was being killed?

2. Meditate on 1 Cor. 13:12.

Simon Tugwell puts it like this: 'So long as we imagine it is we who have been looking for God we can lose heart. But it is the other way round. He has been looking for us.' God has made us in such a way that only His love will fully satisfy our hearts. Husbands, wives, children, families are not enough.

God says He and He alone can meet our deepest longings. But there are problems. God says He loves us, but seemingly He allows bad things to happen to us. He can keep the worlds spinning in space, raise people from the dead, but He won't stop tragedies from entering our lives. How can we give our hearts to a Lover who is so wild, especially when there are other lovers ready to console our hearts? We learn to accept that though God is good, He is not safe. It is a largely a mystery as to how God's glory shines through what we consider to be tragedies. The cross is our only anchor. A God who loves us enough to give His Son for us has to be good. Like Jesus, we can endure anything – as long as we keep our eyes on what lies ahead. Have courage; we'll soon be home.

Father, how thankful I am that I am heading for home. There I shall meet the one who put this romance in my heart and who has opened my eyes to see that what I long for can only be fully met in Him. Come, glorious day. In Jesus' name. Amen.